THE
ALPHA
STRATEGIES

For Jason
Great to meet you

Alan
May 2013

Toronto

THE ALPHA STRATEGIES

UNDERSTANDING STRATEGY, RISK, AND VALUES IN ANY ORGANIZATION

ALAN W. KENNEDY
AND
THOMAS E. KENNEDY

To order additional copies of this book, contact:
Xlibris Corporation
1-888-795-4274
www.Xlibris.com
Orders@Xlibris.com
56189

For
Peter Zarry and Elaine Gutmacher

CONTENTS

ACKNOWLEDGEMENTS

I started teaching for the Schulich Executive Education Centre in 1992. Peter Zarry, the late executive director of SEEC, and his director of operations, Elaine Gutmacher, had been given a mandate to staff the program with consultants rather than tenured academics. Peter's proposition to would-be consultant-teachers was simple: "Fill the seats. Please the seats. Then you get to stay." What Peter failed to mention was the Chinese saying "One teaches. Two learn." I soon fell in love with the learning as well as the teaching. At first, researching and rewriting my principal course, *Strategic Management*, was sufficient. Then I started writing this book.

What with consulting, teaching, researching, and managing the demands of family life, the completion of the project seemed almost impossible at times. Just when I had nearly abandoned hope, my son Tom jumped in to save the day. Over the last two years, he helped me to pull it all together and pushed the book over the finish line for which I will also always be grateful.

I want to thank my readers, especially Professor Alan Middleton, the current executive director of SEEC, for being so supportive of my efforts. Many thanks go as well to David Gibson, John Wallace, Adam Digby, Bud Purves, Brian Sirbovan, David Lehto, Paul Donaldson, Farzin Shahid-Noorai, Ian Kennedy, Bill Digby, Daniel Owen, Michael Lansky, Norm Jarus, Amanda Kennedy, Sarah Kennedy, and Rick Archbold.

I owe a real debt of gratitude to the folks at Kaiser Associates. Twenty years of association with this top tier strategy and competitive research firm has had a great influence on my thinking. The firm's approach to analyzing competitors was what first started me thinking about how to apply the approach to strategy planning.

Many thanks go to Andrew Kennedy for his extraordinary graphics and to Philip Sportel for his art direction. Our editor, John Parry, deserves a special thank-you for his patience and guidance.

My wife, Jo, deserves the most thanks for allowing me to pursue this dream. It has taken far too long. Jo regularly reminds me that I must have every book there is on the subject of strategy from Henri Fayol's wonderful little *General and Industrial Management* (1916) to *Good to Great* (2001) and *Built to Last* (2002) by Jim Collins. Now I can add one more book to the collection.

Alan Kennedy
Toronto, Canada

INTRODUCTION

What if you could

- improve your understanding of your organization's strategy?
- improve your board's understanding of the organization's strategy?
- communicate your strategic plan or business plan on one page?
- show the external factors and risks most impacting strategy?
- be satisfied the most critical risks have been identified?
- improve communication of implementation expectations?
- secure buy-in for the values needed for successful implementation?

The Alpha Strategies provides the framework to achieve all of the above and more. The premise of The Alpha Strategies is that there are eight strategies common to all organizations, whether they are big or small, public sector, for-profit, or not-for-profit.

This simple premise enables the creation of a powerful strategy information capture and presentation table, as shown below.

The Alpha Strategies Framework

THE ALPHA STRATEGIES	
BUSINESS DEFINITION	
RISK	
GROWTH	
FINANCIAL MANAGEMENT	
R+D / TECHNOLOGY	
ORGANIZATION MANAGEMENT	
MARKETING	
SERVICE DELIVERY / PRODUCTION / MANUFACTURING	

Down the left hand column of the table are The Alpha Strategies. Any number of subjects can now be tackled for each strategy. For example, can you describe the actual strategies your organization is using to implement each of The Alpha Strategies? Can you describe the risks and external factors impacting the performance of each of those strategies? Can you describe the values that characterize the implementation of each strategy?

And even if you could provide all those descriptions, do you think your board and management team would agree with you? That's the real power of The Alpha Strategies. The framework enables boards, management, and employees to understand and agree upon current strategy. Understanding current strategy is the critical starting point for all strategy planning.

But what if there was even more to The Alpha Strategies model? What if you could use it to understand:

- the relationships among the eight strategies?
- the culture of the organization?
- the relative roles of each of the strategies?
- the implications of strategy decisions?

We believe that The Alpha Strategies framework can do all these things when converted into the dynamic strategy configuration model shown below. This model enables the relationships among the eight strategies to be seen and discussed.

The Alpha Strategies Dynamic Model

One strategy, which we call the alpha, leads the remaining seven. Two or three of the remaining seven follow immediately behind the alpha. We call these "influencers" because they impose the most guidance and influence on the alpha ahead of them and on the strategies following behind them. The "enablers", consisting of the remaining strategies, form the third category and follow behind the influencers. The choice and configuration of strategies in each organization is what makes organizations unique.

We call the model The Alpha Strategies because all eight are present in all organizations. They are the starting point and the leaders of all strategy in all organizations. Any of the eight can be dominant strategy for the organization as a whole.

Throughout the book, we use real organizations as examples to demonstrate the use of The Alpha Strategies framework and the dynamic strategy configuration model. While we do not expect our readers to agree with all our conclusions, we hope our readers will appreciate how these tools provide the means to begin a focused strategy discussion and to arrive at an informed conclusion.

There are two other matters that readers will notice. The first is the use of the word "strategy". There are almost 750 uses of the word. We hope we can be forgiven for this. After all, this is a book on strategy. We believe the subject of strategy and its planning has been wrapped in mysterious processes and an intimidating vocabulary of synonyms and buzz words for strategy for too long. We refuse to use synonyms for strategy. We just use the word strategy. The second matter is the use of the pronouns "I" and "We". When the reader sees the use of "I", it means that the example or opinion comes from Alan's teaching or consulting experience. "We", of course, means the shared opinion of the authors.

Our sincere hope is that The Alpha Strategies makes the subject more accessible and enables board members, management, and employees to take their organizations to new levels of performance excellence.

For more information on The Alpha Strategies, visit us at:

WWW.THEALPHASTRATEGIES.COM

CHAPTER 1
THE ALPHA STRATEGIES

Eight Strategies Common to All Organizations

There is a framework of eight strategies that is common to all for-profit, not-for-profit, and public sector organizations, regardless of their size.

We call the framework The Alpha Strategies because the alphas are the starting point and the leaders of all strategy in all organizations.

All eight are present in all organizations. They are the pillars on which all strategic planning and subsequent strategy implementation planning are founded.

Figure 1 Eight Strategies Common to All Organizations

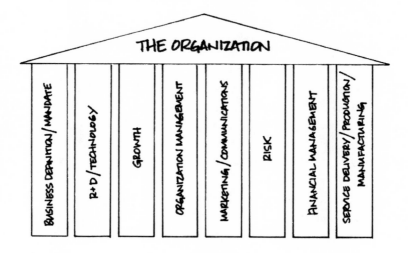

The eight alpha strategies are business definition, financial management, growth, marketing, organization management, research and development / technology, risk, and service delivery / manufacturing / production.

For not-for-profits and public sector organizations, business definition is called the mandate and marketing is known as communications. Service delivery is also called production or manufacturing depending on the nature of an organization's business.

A reader's first reaction to this list of strategies should be that the list looks familiar. It is familiar. We bump up against these strategies every day at work. Every organization has all eight. We typically see them as functions or departments. What organization doesn't have a finance group, marketing (or communications group), risk function, human resources, R&D, IT or technology group, and a service delivery group? This last function is also known as manufacturing or production depending on what your organization does.

As for growth, that strategy is usually managed in departments such as "land use planning" in municipalities or "business development", "corporate development", and "the acquisitions group" in most other organizations.

Business definition, or "mandate" as it is called in public sector organizations, is the responsibility of the board of directors or council or whatever the highest decision making body might be called in an organization because the business definition or interpretation of the mandate sets the boundaries for the activities the organization is prepared to undertake.

Human nature makes us want to test the list of strategies by seeing if it relates to our reality. Our reality is what we do in our job. Where does my job fit into the strategy framework? "Am I in the finance function? Or maybe my job is in the service delivery group?" These are the sorts of questions that make the strategy framework become very real because your job can be found in one of the eight strategies.

Now, look around a bit more widely to where you might find these eight strategies. In business schools, they represent the basic subjects taught. Publicly traded companies are required to address all eight, in one form or another, in their disclosure filings. Competitive researchers and industry analysts typically organize their research on a target company by addressing all of these strategies. In other words, the eight are all around us all the time.

The concept of a common framework of strategies is not new. Henri Fayol identified six of the eight in *General and Industrial Management* (1916). His book is arguably the first book ever written on the newly emerging subject of business strategy and its management. Peter Drucker identified the remaining two some forty years later in *The Practice of Management* (1954).

We see the framework being used all around us. But it is not being used to facilitate better strategic and business planning. We think the time has come to start using it for that purpose.

Strategy is a Choice of a Course of Action

We are proposing that there are eight strategies (courses of action) that all organizations must address. Therefore, we believe that all of The Alpha Strategies are indeed strategies.

A typical comment I get from attendees in my courses is: "Not all eight 'feel like' strategies." For example, some folks believe organization management can only play a supporting role and is never, in their opinion, a "strategy".

The fact is that the vocabulary for strategy is typically different in every organization. If I say to a group that I want to talk about strategy, I watch the group start to get tense. This is happening because everyone in the group has her or his own idea of what does and does not constitute strategy. Unfortunately, we see all of this divergence of opinion on the basic language of strategy as creating a very real problem for strategy communication and understanding.

The conventional approach to the strategy vocabulary is to use some sort of variation on terms such as purpose, goals, mission, vision, objectives, strategies, and tactics. We do not subscribe to this overly cumbersome approach. We think all of these terms are simply synonyms for strategy and we believe strategy is quite simply a chosen course of action.

If you look at all the various terms, the fundamental distinguishing characteristic among them is the implied time frame for implementation associated with each term. For example, vision is distinguished by a long time frame. Tactics are distinguished by a very short time frame.

But between the lack of a common understanding on what that implied time frame might be and the lack of a meaningful definition for each term, we think the current strategy vocabulary has become a major barrier to effective strategy communications. How many readers have wasted time in meetings debating whether they are talking about a strategy or an objective or a tactic? It is as though learning the manufactured differences for a bunch of synonyms for strategy becomes more important than understanding what action is required.

The greatest weakness in the current practice of focusing on a framework of synonyms is that it takes our attention away from the real issue; being a discussion on the choices of action.

Therefore, we offer our activity focused definition of strategy. We believe strategy should be defined as a chosen course of action.

We believe that there are eight strategies (courses of action) that all organizations must address. Therefore, we believe that all of The Alpha Strategies are indeed strategies.

The way we suggest one strategy can be distinguished from another is by giving it a time frame and identifying the core activity being addressed. Using this approach, for example, we would talk about our five year marketing strategy, our first quarter growth strategy, our three month communications strategy, our three year service delivery strategy, and so on. This makes clear both the subject of the strategy and the time frame for its implementation. This approach also eliminates the need to use synonyms for strategy.

We are not suggesting that organizations do away with their lexicons for strategy although we think it would certainly expedite better strategy understanding and communication if they did. What we are proposing is a means for individuals to decipher the confusing strategy language of their organization. Individuals should focus on identifying and understanding the core activity and implementation time frame for the actions being discussed and ignore whether the action is being called a "goal" or a "strategic objective" or whatever. That label is not useful information.

The Alpha Strategies are indeed strategies. They are clearly long term choices of action when they are used in the strategic plan. Each subsequent implementation of each of the alphas results in shorter and shorter implementation time frames.

For example, say the long term marketing strategy of a start-up technology firm is to be in all major global markets. The five year marketing strategy of the start-up might be to become established in Europe and North America. The three year marketing strategy might be to become established in North America. The one year marketing strategy might be to become established in the United States. The first quarter marketing strategy might be to target the most attractive markets on the U.S. east coast.

Armed with this explanation of strategy, let's take a closer look at the eight strategies. A brief description of each of The Alpha Strategies is as follows:

Business Definition / Mandate
Business definition, referred to as mandate in not-for-profit and public sector organizations, focuses on the positioning of the organization within the context of the external environment. Not-for-profits and public sector organizations are given a general description of that positioning in their enabling legislation or charter of incorporation. Business definition or mandate is the basis of the mission statements found in many organizations.

Financial Management
Financial management focuses on the sourcing, allocation, and management of financial capital and all other aspects of management of the organization's finances.

Growth
Growth focuses on the type and rate of the organization's growth. This may involve the organization's expansion, staying the same size, becoming smaller, or even ceasing to exist.

Marketing / Communications

Marketing, referred to as communications in not-for-profit and public sector organizations, focuses on identifying and capturing customers and clients with the promise of value that will be delivered in the organization's goods and services.

Organization Management

Organization management relates to the sourcing, allocation, and management of human capital, being the personnel requirements of the firm.

R&D / Technology

R&D / technology focuses on how the organization leverages technology. This can be as sophisticated as how a big pharmaceutical firm produces a new drug or as straight forward as the decision to upgrade the phone system.

Risk

Risk focuses on the identification and management of the possible occurrence of the unacceptable; being threats to the success of the organization as a whole.

Service Delivery / Manufacturing / Production

Service delivery focuses on delivering the services promised by the marketing or communications message. In some organizations, the strategy is known as manufacturing or as production.

The Eight Choices of Action

A more detailed discussion of each of the eight strategies is now provided.

Marketing / Communications

Marketing, or communications as it is known for not-for-profits and in the public sector, focuses on identifying demand (called the "need" in public sector not-for-profit parlance) for the organization's services, products, or programs, and capturing that demand. As such, the marketing strategy includes the sales process.

In my courses, students ask how business definition differs from marketing. "Aren't they the same thing?" is the usual question. They are very different. The difference lies in the focus of each. Business definition (or mandate) positions the organization as a whole within the external environment. Marketing, in contrast, focuses on a different question, which Drucker framed as: "What does the customer consider value?"

For purposes of The Alpha Strategies, marketing includes sales and spans the range of activities from identifying products and markets to be sold through framing the message of value, pricing, and quality for products and services, selecting marketing channels to promote the product, and selling the product.

The issue inherent in marketing is best shown in the following matrix, which shows customers/markets being balanced with the selection of products and services.

Figure 2 Major Marketing / Communications Issues

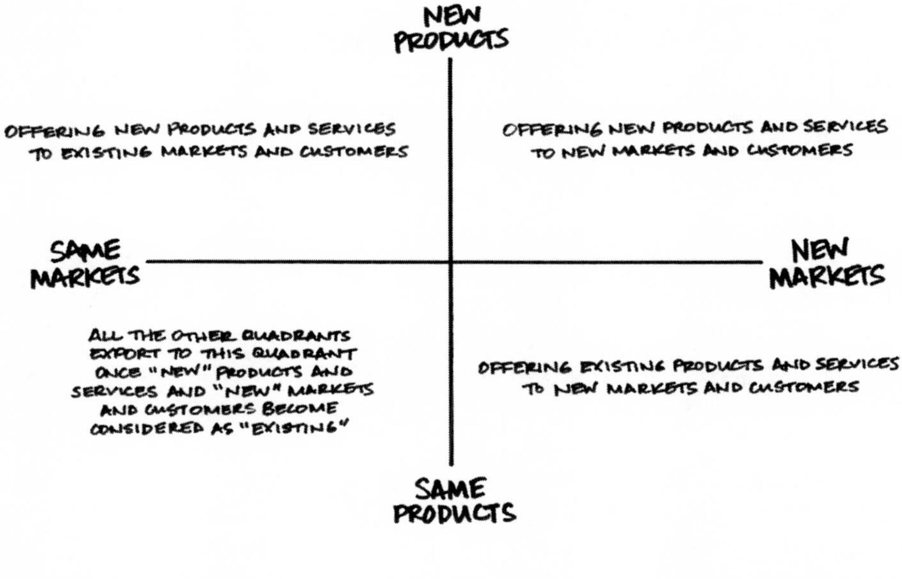

NEW
PRODUCTS

OFFERING NEW PRODUCTS AND SERVICES
TO EXISTING MARKETS AND CUSTOMERS

OFFERING NEW PRODUCTS AND SERVICES
TO NEW MARKETS AND CUSTOMERS

SAME
MARKETS

NEW
MARKETS

ALL THE OTHER QUADRANTS
EXPORT TO THIS QUADRANT
ONCE "NEW" PRODUCTS AND
SERVICES AND "NEW" MARKETS
AND CUSTOMERS BECOME
CONSIDERED AS "EXISTING"

OFFERING EXISTING PRODUCTS AND SERVICES
TO NEW MARKETS AND CUSTOMERS

SAME
PRODUCTS

Every organization starts its marketing in the bottom left hand quadrant. As a result, this is the quadrant of existing or same products/services being offered to existing or same markets/customers. The question is "Where do we go next?" as the firm grows or needs to change to address a changing external environment.

The choices for answering the question "Where do we go next" are displayed in the upper left, lower right, and upper right quadrants.

In the upper left quadrant, we can offer new products and services to existing markets/customers. In the lower right quadrant, we can offer our presently existing products/services in new markets to new customers.

Finally, there is the most challenging quadrant of all, namely the upper right. In this quadrant, we are offering new products and services in new markets to new customers. The challenge in this quadrant arises because of the learning curve implicit in successfully understanding and addressing both the needs of new customers and markets and the challenges of launching new products and services developed to meet those needs.

Directors and senior management should be aware how marketing is being positioned within this matrix as a starting place for understanding marketing within their organization. They should also be aware that, at some point, the logic of the matrix is that successful entry into any of three quadrants other than the lower left quadrant will eventually move back into the lower left and become what constitutes existing or same products and services and existing or same customers and markets.

In other words, the other three quadrants should always be adding to the lower left over time. The question becomes "When is 'new' no longer 'new'?" At some point, the "new" converts to "existing" and becomes a part of the lower left quadrant offering of existing products and services to existing markets and customers.

My courses are invariably attended by a mix of public sector, not-for-profit, and private sector attendees. As a result, a typical comment I hear from the folks in the not-for-profits and public sector organizations is "But we don't market."

I respond with, "Fine. Then change the name "marketing" to "communications" and tell me if that feels better." Every organization has to manage the perception of value and relevance it delivers. This is done by conveying messages of value and relevance to stakeholders and target markets. The premise of marketing and of communications is the same. The goal is to capture attention and commitment.

Financial Management

Financial management addresses the sourcing, allocation, and management of financial capital and management of the organization's finances.

Financial management is generally well understood. Folks have been managing money a long time.

The sophistication of that understanding is evident in the number of authorities around the world granting financial designations.

These include the chartered accountant (CA), chartered financial analyst (CFA), certified general accountant (CGA), certified management accountant (CMA), and certified public accountant (CPA), to say nothing of the dozens and dozens of lesser known but equally rigorous professional financial designations.

Financial management is usually thought of as a tool for control of an organization's finances.

From keeping proper records and preparing proper financial reporting and statements to conducting financial audits, financial management is a mainstay of control.

Invariably, studies of the collapse of organizations reveal lack of financial controls as a major contributing factor.

But financial management is broader than being just a tool of control.

It can also help enhance financial performance. Decisions on accounting, sources of capital, tax planning, capital structuring, and so on can substantially affect an organization's performance.

The issue inherent in financial management is shown in the following matrix. The issue is finding the right balance between performance enhancement and control of the organization's finances.

Figure 3 Financial Management Issues

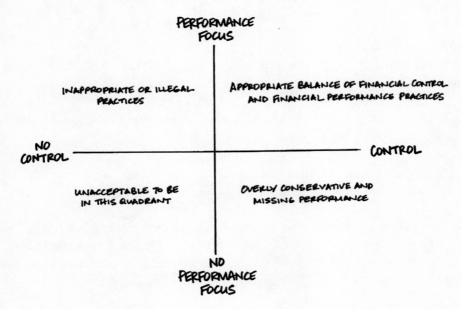

If there are too few controls, such as record keeping and auditing, the possibility for inappropriate activity increases. Too much focus on performance, such as using aggressive tax or accounting practices to bolster results, can also become problematic.

Service Delivery / Production / Manufacturing
Service delivery, which includes production and manufacturing, focuses on the creation of the output that marketing promises.

Service delivery firms would include those providing consulting or policing services. Most car companies are characterized as manufacturers. The big oil and gas producers and the world's biggest gold miners are examples of production companies.

The service delivery strategy includes all the inputs needed to produce and deliver a finished product, together with such promised post completion obligations, such as warranties.

The issue inherent in service delivery / production / manufacturing is achieving better productivity.

Productivity is a result of the right blend of efficiency and effectiveness. Too much focus on effectiveness and efficiency can be lost. On the other hand, if there is too much focus on efficiency, then it is the other way around; effectiveness can be lost.

Figure 4 Service Delivery / Production / Manufacturing Issues

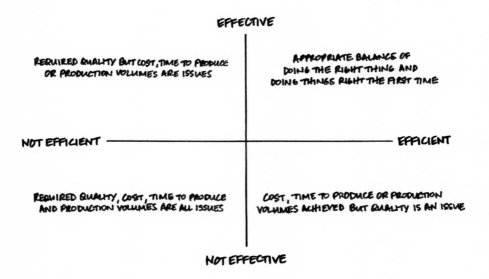

It would seem common sense that the upper right hand quadrant is the one that seems the most appropriate for all organizations. Obviously, it is harder to achieve the balance of doing the right thing and doing things right than it looks. For example, where might the balance be between effectiveness and efficiency when a life hangs in the balance, as is the case with the delivery of many hospital services?

As with marketing, there is a sizeable body of knowledge surrounding service delivery / manufacturing / production. It is the one strategy of the eight that is most strongly associated with process improvement methodologies as the way to improve productivity. From ISO certification methods, through lean manufacturing to Hoshin Planning, Six Sigma, and the Toyota Way, to name a few of the better known methods, the service delivery / production / manufacturing stands ahead of the other seven alphas in its use of techniques to improve strategy implementation through better understanding and constant improvement of implementation processes.

We are of the opinion that one of the trends of the next decade will be the application of those improvement methodologies to the other seven strategies as the means to improve productivity across all The Alpha Strategies.

Organization Management

Organization management focuses on sourcing, allocating, and managing the organization's personnel. As such, it includes identifying the skills to manage the requirements of the other alphas, finding people with the right skills and experience to address those requirements, and helping to manage and develop those people.

The Alpha Strategies model provides the starting point for reviewing organizational design. To demonstrate this, look at the chart depicting your organization's top level management. You should be able to track each senior position back to one of the eight strategies. If there is a strategy with no apparent management assigned to it, then I would suggest that the gap needs to be addressed.

For example, you will probably find that the management of the risk is buried somewhere under another strategy, usually financial management, rather than being a stand-alone responsibility comparable in importance to financial management and the other seven alphas.

On that note, one of the more encouraging current management trends is the practice of appointing a "chief" for more than just the CEO (chief executive officer), COO (chief operating officer), and CFO (chief financial officer) roles. There are now organizations with chief marketing officers, chief people officers, chief risk officers, and chief technology officers. This trend seems perfectly consistent with our thinking that large organizations have, at least intuitively, recognized the importance of managing each of The Alpha Strategies.

Of course, in a small organization, the owner typically assumes responsibility for managing all eight strategies. This is why I think employees of small organizations get so baffled when talking to the boss. They can never be sure which hat (being used here as a metaphor for each of The Alpha Strategies) the owner/boss is wearing when talking to them.

It should come as no surprise that we think the issue inherent in organization management turns on whether strategy is understood and being followed throughout the organization, as shown in the following matrix.

Figure 5 Organization Management Issues

In other words, organization management turns on the balance between "walking the walk" (taking action on the agreed strategy) and "talking the talk" (talking about the agreed strategy).

How many organizations do you know that you think are located in the bottom right hand quadrant?

The big question, of course, is whether your own organization is in that quadrant. These organizations are characterized by the fact that what they say is not what they do.

Boards have the responsibility to understand the strategies they are being asked to approve and to monitor their implementation.

Boards should be ever vigilant, looking for disconnects between what is being said and what is actually being done. This is the essence of governance and oversight.

Growth

Growth focuses on the type and rate of an organization's growth. Growth can also include no growth and shrinking.

There are two types of basic growth strategies. The choices are basically to grow internally from the ever growing demand for the organization's products and services or to grow externally through acquisitions, mergers, franchising, licensing arrangements, partnerships, and joint ventures.

Internal growth is a consequence of success in marketing and producing the organization's services and products. The customer keeps coming back for more and the number of customers keeps growing. Negative internal growth could result from the orderly winding down of under-performing product and service lines or withdrawal from certain unattractive markets.

External growth often provides a means to accelerate growth even faster than internal growth might allow. Negative external growth could result from the divestiture of certain assets or operations that are considered to be non-core or an unattractive use of the organization's resources.

The challenge with either internal or external growth is whether management understands the consequences of that growth on managing the company. Growth means change. Unless management is actively managing the change driven by growth, management could lose control of the organization.

The issue inherent in the growth strategy, as shown in the drawing below, is the rate of growth as balanced with the type of growth. Internal growth is usually slower than growth by acquisitions, although there are plenty of examples otherwise.

Figure 6 Growth Issues

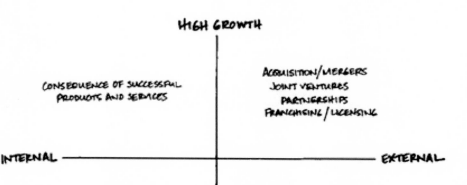

The issue inherent in the bottom left hand would seem to be whether or not the organization intends to grow at all. In the bottom right hand quadrant, the issue might be a flawed implementation of the external growth strategy. There is no growth in spite of acquisitions or other forms of external growth strategies.

The upper left hand quadrant is the result of the successful internal growth strategy resulting from successful marketing and delivery of products and services. The upper right hand quadrant reflects the successful use of acquisitions or other forms of external growth.

Research & Development / Technology

Research and development / technology relates to development and use of proprietary and intellectual property for competitive advantage or as an enabler or both. The development of that intellectual property comes through research and development. That intellectual property might be technology. For this reason, it seems appropriate to us to bundle research and development with technology to form a single strategy.

The issue inherent in R&D / technology is the choice between the elements (i.e., either R&D or technology or both) for competitive advantage or for enabling productivity or both.

Figure 7 R&D / technology Issues

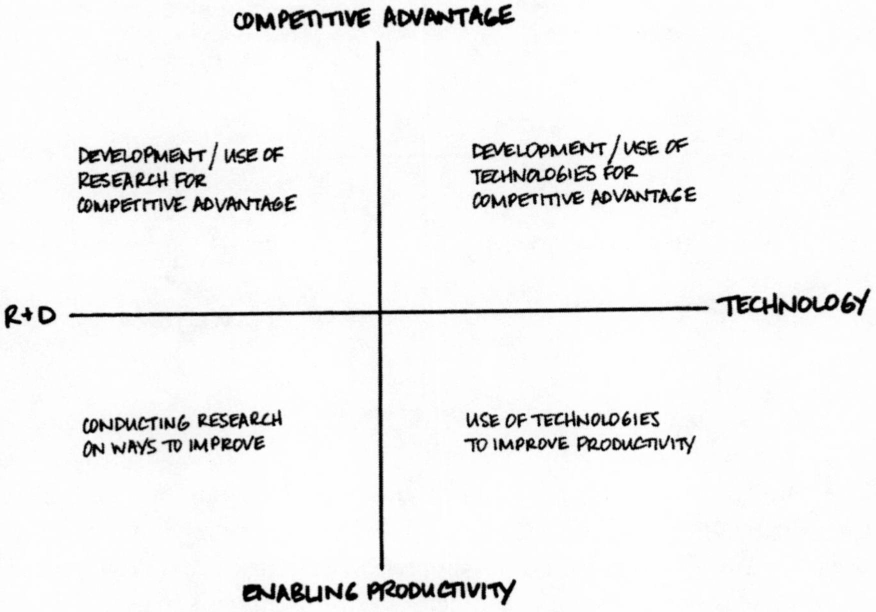

The bottom right and left hand quadrants reflect the most typical use of the strategy. Most organizations will find themselves in the bottom right hand quadrant because they are using technology to enable productivity. They may not have developed the technology themselves. But the technology they are using, say, in the form of computers, cell phones, and so on, enables productivity.

Some organizations also conduct sufficient research on ways to produce productivity that they could be considered to be in the bottom left hand quadrant. Toyota comes to mind with all of the research it has done developing "The Toyota Way" of production processes.

The upper left hand and right hand quadrants represent the use of research and development and of technology for competitive advantage. In the upper left hand quadrant, the quality of the organization's research output gives it competitive advantage. Sometimes the output is technology. Many times it is not.

In the upper right hand quadrant, the organization is using technology for competitive advantage. The technology may have been developed through the organization's research and development efforts (i.e., through work occurring in the upper left hand quadrant). It may also have been purchased from a third party.

Risk
Risk is defined as a focus on the possible occurrence of the unacceptable, which, for us, includes missing opportunities. Risk has only recently come into its own as a strategy, notwithstanding its early identification as one of the eight common to all organizations. This is because risk has been seen, in the past, as an insurance or legal matter.

The insurance industry is one of the oldest industries there is. The practice of risk transference (paying an insurer a fee to take the liability for a risk) worked well, as a strategy, until the 1980s. Buying insurance was the risk strategy. By the end of the twentieth century, risks included environmental and ethical matters, as well as unacceptable business practices, which ranged from the use of child labor, to pay inequity and discrimination. Risks also now included terrorism and a whole host of other outcomes of doing business in a shrinking world. Risk was no longer something that could be solely or easily addressed by insurance. Risk had become a strategy to be managed.

As for treating risk as a legal matter, this is an expensive and reactive approach. Lawyers would rather manage the fallout after a risk occurrence. And why not? The profession knows that human nature is to do whatever it takes in a crisis. After all, clients are not willing to spend money preparing for something that might never happen and are prepared to spend whatever it takes when it does.

The issues inherent in the risk strategy are shown in the following matrix. The probability must be balanced with the consequences of occurrence.

Figure 8 Risk Issues

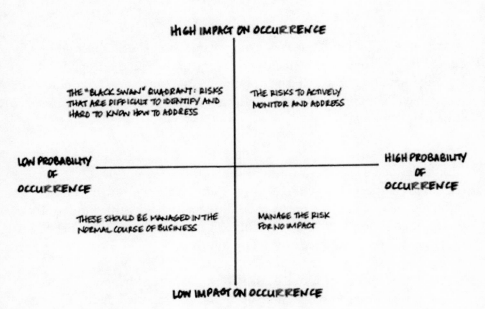

The upper right hand quadrant of risks with a high probability of occurrence and high impact are the ones that on which most organizations focus. These are identifiable risks that must be managed either by avoiding the risk all altogether, transferring the risk to a third party, such as an insurer, or managing the risk and trying to minimize either the probability of occurrence or consequences.

The bottom left hand and right hand quadrants represent scenarios that management should be expected to manage in the normal course of business.

However, it is the upper left hand quadrant that is the most problematic. This is because of the high impact on occurrence but low probability. This quadrant is the one that Nassim Nicholas Taleb explores in his best-selling book, *The Black Swan: The Impact of the Highly Improbable* (2007).

This is the quadrant in which we would place the grounding and capsizing of the huge cruise ship, Costa Concordia, off the coast of Italy in January 2012. The tragedy occurred allegedly because the captain felt the need to show-off to friends watching on shore how close he could take the massive vessel to the shoreline. How could the cruise company have foreseen that risk? The unbelievably horrific events of 9/11 would also fit into the upper left quadrant as would arguably the BP Deepwater Horizon oil rig explosion and pollution event in the Gulf of Mexico in 2010.

The common characteristic for all of the upper left hand quadrant risks is the catastrophic consequences which cannot be ignored. But the reality is that these risks were ignored because the effort required to address them seemed impossible to mount.

Business Definition / Mandate

Business definition, or mandate, describes how the organization has positioned itself within the external environment. It is best known, in current planning parlance, as the mission statement, although many mission statements go far beyond what is required to describe mandate or positioning.

Peter Drucker identified the strategy in *The Practice of Management* (1954), when he famously asked: "What is our business and what should it be?" Drucker's simple question took on a life of its own in the ensuing fifty plus years. Drucker intended the question to force managers to understand how customers and clients saw their business.

Bruce Henderson, founder of Boston Consulting Group (BCG), the global American management consulting firm, seized on the idea in the early 1960s and built an immensely successful organization by offering research services to provide that information. Even today, Henderson's basic research methodology is still evident in BCG research studies. Henderson "got it." Drucker was in effect saying, "Take an outside-in look at your business. Look at yourself through the eyes of your customer."

Unfortunately, it takes a lot of work and a strong stomach to see yourself the way customers, clients, competitors, or users, see you. They won't always agree that you are doing the great job you think you are doing. Outsiders can be brutally honest, leaving a manager wincing from the feedback.

By 1982, John Pearce published his now famous article, *The Company Mission as a Strategic Tool,* in the *Harvard Business Review*. The piece seems to have touched off an explosion in the popularity of the "inside-out" approach to answering the question, "What is our business and what should it be?" Instead of spending effort determining how customers and clients see the business as the means to frame the business definition strategy, the consulting industry seized on Pearce's idea as the means to have clients look at themselves, not as customers or clients would, but instead as how the clients wanted to see themselves. The inside-out approach to planning and mission statement development was born.

The issue inherent in business definition (known as "mandate" for most not-for-profits and public sector organizations) is the balance of "how do we compete", being on value or on price, with "where do we compete," being either a narrow, highly focused definition of where the organization competes versus a much broader definition.

As shown in the matrix below, the horizontal axis moves from "Narrow" to "Broad". This represents the basic choice an organization makes in deciding whether it is going to offer a narrow range of products and services or a broad range. The vertical axis represents the choice between competing on price (meaning offering the lowest price available for the firm's products and services) and competing on the value of those products and services (in the opinion of the organization's customers / clients / users).

Figure 9 Business Definition Issues

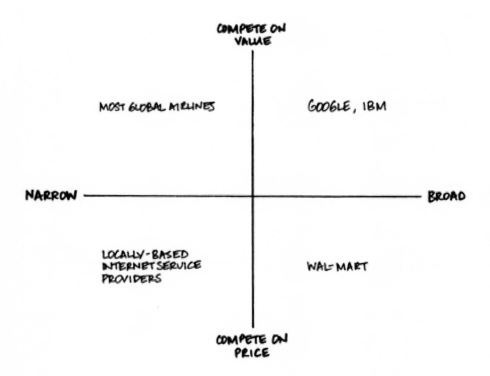

In the private sector, Wal-Mart Stores Inc., the giant retailer, would be found in the lower right hand quadrant. Wal-Mart competes on a promise to offer the lowest prices possible. Wal-Mart competes broadly, being a multinational corporation, and offering products and services from groceries to apparel, home electronics, automotive, health and wellness, jewelry, music, outdoor living, appliances, toys, and more.

Firms in the upper right hand quadrant compete broadly and on value. Representative firms include IBM, which focuses on high value information technology products and services, and Google, the ubiquitous Internet search firm which aims to organize the world's data.

The upper left hand quadrant is filled with firms that compete on the basis of value but are narrower in their focus than firms in the right hand quadrant. For example, some national and international airlines might be found in the upper left hand quadrant if they compete on value and not on price and have a narrow service offering of only airline travel. The lower left hand quadrant is for narrowly focused firms such as locally based Internet service providers who try to compete on price.

For public sector and not-for-profit organizations, the issue of positioning of the organization is addressed in the enabling statute or charter of the organization. Therefore, these organizations do not have the flexibility of for-profits in the setting of this strategy or changing it.

Most public sector and not-for-profits compete on value rather than price. The thinking behind this notion is that the services they provide cannot attract the interest of the private sector. This is because there are usually low financial returns or high risks associated with those activities. Or, the activity is thought to be an inappropriate service to be delivered by the private sector because the motivation for profits will negatively impact delivery of the service.

Do You Know the Eight Strategies of Your Organization?

Do you, as a board member or a member of the management team, know your organization's eight strategies? Could you write down a description of the marketing strategy? How about financial management, growth, business definition, organization management, R&D / technology, service delivery, and risk? If your answer is "Yes, I could!", then the question becomes "Do you think the entire management team and the board of directors would agree with your descriptions?" I expect, in most cases, the answer would be a "No!"

We are constantly surprised to see organizations engaging in strategic planning without decision makers having a common understanding of what constitutes current strategy. How can strategic planning begin without agreement on a description of current strategy? The pervasive belief is that the process starts with the question "Where do we want to be?" rather than the more logical "Where are we?"

This is why we believe The Alpha Strategies are the starting point for all strategic planning.

How can change to any of the eight strategies be recommended if there is not a common understanding of those strategies? Today's planning practices typically start with the suspect assumption that decision makers fully understand current strategy and how it is being implemented. This means most planning starts with presentations on the need for change and the recommended strategy to address that need.

Ask yourself this. When was the last time you attended a strategic planning session and the starting point was a detailed discussion of current strategy aimed at ensuring that all decision makers present had the same understanding of it? The answer is more likely than not, never. At best, there might have been a high level, cursory assessment of the organization's "strengths" and "weaknesses". Or maybe the "core competencies" or prior year's results were reviewed.

The point is that this very broad current state assessment was based on the assumption that there is a common understanding of the organization's strategies and how they are being implemented. Or worse, the assumption is that decision makers, such as board members, do not need to understand current strategy in order to review and approve management recommended changes to strategy. This would represent a serious weakness in governance.

We call this type of strategic planning the "want-to-be" approach. The focus is on the more exciting subject of what we should do to achieve a bright, hoped for future that comes from proposed strategy rather than spending time on the hard realities that come from truly understanding today's strategies and their performance.

Want-to-be planning usually quickly moves to creating visions and missions or stretch, heroic, and audacious goals, all without a common understanding of current strategy. As a result, many vision and mission statements prepared as a result of this process are either so vague as to be meaningless or can seem almost verging on being delusional about the abilities of the organization.

More disturbingly, want-to-be planning usually focuses on only two or maybe three of the eight strategies without having undertaken the due diligence necessary to confirm that the strategies chosen for change are the right ones of the eight on which to focus. Needless to say, there is rarely consideration of the impact of the proposed change on the remaining strategies.

The Alpha Strategies provides the starting point for fact based planning.

The approach enables boards and management to capture descriptions of present strategies, risks to those strategies that are impacting their performance, and the current values that characterize strategy implementation.

Once boards and management are in agreement on those facts, they can then begin to discuss what changes, if any, are warranted because of uncontrollable factors in a changing external environment.

CHAPTER 2
THE ALPHA STRATEGIES: A DYNAMIC MODEL

The Dynamic Nature of The Alpha Strategies

The Alpha Strategies model is not just a static listing of eight strategies. It is also a dynamic model.

Not only are each of The Alpha Strategies unique to each organization, the positioning of those strategies in relation to one another is unique to every organization.

A depiction of the dynamic model can be seen in the figure below.

Figure 10 The Dynamic Model of The Alpha Strategies

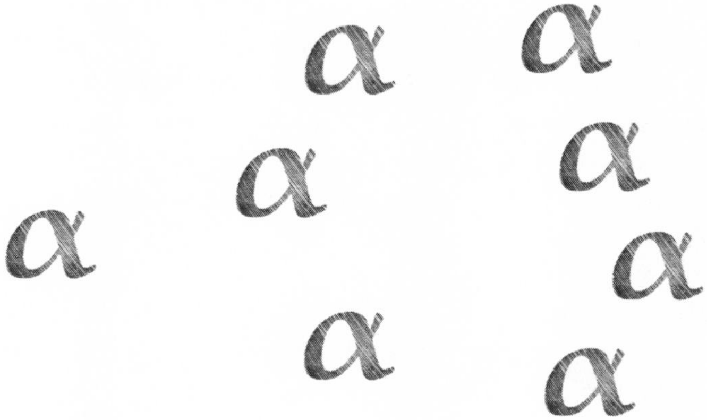

The model assumes that there is always one strategy leading all the others. We call this lead strategy, "alpha". The other seven strategies follow closely behind.

An important aspect of understanding current strategy requires understanding which strategy leads the organization and how the remaining strategies are organized behind it.

The Alpha Strategies model assumes that strategies can move from their present positions to new positions in the configuration as a consequence of decisions made on strategy.

As a result, a powerful aspect of the model is that it makes it possible to "see" the impact that a decision on one strategy could have on the remaining seven and how relative positions of strategies could change as a result of that decision.

The idea of a dynamic model of multiple strategies is not new.

Benjamin Tregoe and John Zimmerman described a dynamic model of strategy in their classic, *Top Management Strategy: What It Is and How to Make It Work* (1980). Tregoe and Zimmerman believed there were eight potential driving forces (their name for strategies) at the core of any organization. Their model focused mainly on what products and services the organization should offer and the markets and customers it should serve. Because of this, their model did not address business definition / mandate, growth, organization management, or risk.

The idea for The Alpha Strategies model came from a cartoon I saw long ago in The New Yorker magazine. It showed a school of seven or eight fish with lead fish labeled "CEO". No doubt, the followers were the CEO's management team. In keeping with the dry wit that so characterizes New Yorker cartoons, there was no caption. There are plenty of possibilities. Maybe the cartoonist believed executive management is all wet or is a group of cold fish.

Whatever the intent of the drawing, the image of the school of fish swimming through a changing environment and lead by one of the fish struck me as an excellent metaphor for the dynamic nature of strategy.

We believe that dominant or lead strategy is present in every organization. We are also going to argue that this lead strategy is very difficult to change and stays in place for long periods of time.

Once again, the concept of dominant strategy is not new. Tregoe and Zimmerman called it the "Driving Force".

It was Canada's own world-class strategic thinker and prolific author, Dr. Henry Mintzberg who, with Dr. James A. Waters, studied the strategies of the Quebec based grocery retailing chain, Steinberg's, over a sixty year period. See: *Tracking Strategy in an Entrepreneurial Firm* (Academy of Management Journal; Sept 1982, Vol. 25 Issue 3, p. 465-499). They concluded that strategic direction, which we believe is set by the lead strategy, remains unchanged over long periods of time and that strategy is very difficult to change.

We are also going to propose that changing the lead strategy of an organization is very difficult because it represents the dominant culture of that organization. And we all know how difficult it is to change a culture.

As a result, we believe that understanding current strategy goes beyond simply being able to describe, in detail, each of The Alpha Strategies. The strategies are also dynamic. It is also necessary to understand how current strategies are configured. This means understanding which strategy is leading the remaining seven and how the remaining seven are organized behind that lead strategy.

Alpha, Influencers, and Enablers

Our research on the strategies of for-profit, not-for-profit, and public sector organizations over the last ten years leads us to believe that the eight strategies of The Alpha Strategies fall into three categories. They are the alpha, influencer, and enabler categories.

Only one strategy is in the alpha or lead strategy category.

Two, or maybe three, are in the influencer category.

The remaining strategies are in the enabler category.

The typical configuration of strategy looks as follows:

Figure 11 The Model Showing Alpha, Influencers, and Enablers

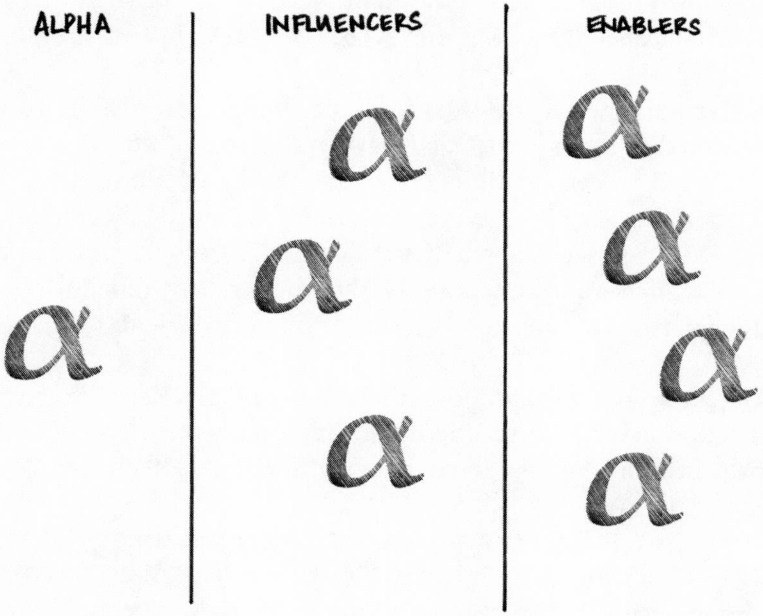

A question I often get asked in my courses is "What's the significance of my job being in a strategy at the back of the pack? Does being in an enabling strategy rather than being close to the lead strategy or being in the lead strategy make my enabler strategy less important?"

The answer is that all eight of The Alpha Strategies must be well executed in order for the organization itself to be high performing.

How many organizations can you name that, for example, had growth as the lead only to collapse into ruin because they could not manage their finances or production or risk?

If all eight are not high performing, the organization cannot achieve high performance. The fact that your job is found in an enabler strategy rather than the alpha or an influencer does not make your job any less important. If your strategy does not perform, it will hobble the organization.

We can usually fairly quickly identify the lead or alpha strategy because it is reflected in the dominant culture of the organization.

The influencers are identifiable as the two or three strategies that seem to exert the most guidance and constraint on both the alpha and on the enablers.

For example, we have noted that financial management (when it is not alpha, of course) is very often an influencer. What this means to us is that the alpha strategy will be constrained by the requirements of the financial management strategy. Similarly, the financial management strategy imposes guidance and constraints on the enablers.

The enablers are the remaining strategies. In some ways, the enablers are almost as easy to identify as the alpha because they are identified through a process of elimination. Once the alpha is identified, the remaining strategies become candidates for being influencers. Those that are not found to be influencers are the enablers. Enablers can impact performance of the organization if they are not high performing. But assuming they are high performing, they have no other influence.

For example, information technology is an enabler in many organizations. If growth was the alpha, then I.T. would be expected to deliver scalability and to keep ahead of the usual pressures growth imposes when it is alpha. But I.T. would not have any influence on growth except if I.T. stumbled and couldn't deliver high performance, thereby impairing the growth initiative. Individual enablers may not have the influence of the alpha or the influencers, but the failure of any one of them to deliver can sure drag down the performance of the entire organization just as if they were the alpha or one of the influencers.

Our premise is that alpha is readily identifiable (once you know how to look for it) because it sets the culture for the organization as a whole. We all know, intuitively at least, that there are organizations known for their service ability or financial abilities or growth, or risk management, or marketing, or technology. We are moving beyond the intuitive and trying to explain why those firms are perceived that way.

At first this may seem like a challenging concept. But look around at organizations, particularly large ones, and it is possible to see the alpha or lead strategy. Consider Coca-Cola, Nike, and Pepsi. They are all known as quintessential marketing firms. Their distinguishing strength is marketing. Their culture is marketing. Their alpha is clearly marketing.

Look at government organizations. Most are in the business of delivering services, be they at the municipal, county, regional, provincial, state, or federal levels of government. Their alpha is service delivery. But then there are many other government organizations that have the responsibility to regulate, making risk their alpha.

Consider the story of Isadore Sharp, founder of the Four Seasons hotels chain. In his book, *Four Season: The Story of a Business Philosophy* (2009), Sharp writes that he had no vision for his business. Yet he also says he was obsessed with service excellence, something which became the hallmark of all his properties and differentiated his hotel chain from all competitors. Sharp clearly made service excellence (the service delivery strategy) his company's alpha and he relentlessly pursued it.

We think each organization's choice of strategy configuration (i.e., how the eight strategies are positioned in the three categories) and the specific choices of strategy for each is what truly makes every organization unique.

And we think that the alpha strategy sets the culture for an organization.

On hearing this description of alpha, one of the first questions I hear in my executive education courses is "Can there be more than one alpha strategy leading the organization?"

My answer is "No." In any plan, there can only be one alpha strategy.

It takes years and years for an alpha strategy to take hold, to become the leader, and to set the culture for the organization. If there were competing alphas, say growth and marketing, the organization would become dysfunctional because of the confusion over the conflicting strategic priorities. This confusion is usually reflected by questions such as "What is our first priority? Is it growth or is it marketing?"

This is why it is so important for the board and the CEO to understand which strategy is alpha or dominant strategy.

We can cite examples of CEOs who struggled with the companies they were hired to run simply because they never understood the culture of the organization. This means to us that they did not know which strategy was alpha.

For example, imagine trying to manage a retailer, having marketing as its alpha, as though financial management was the dominant strategy. In other words, imagine trying to turn marketing types into numbers guys.

Or imagine an organization with risk as its dominant strategy being managed as though service delivery was its alpha. In other words, imagine trying to turn border customs inspections officers into customer service representatives!

This dysfunction or confusion over alpha can also be seen in organizations trying to implement a change to their alpha strategy. Changing or replacing the alpha is not easy because it can take years and years to embed the new strategy and its related culture or way of doing business.

Research in Motion (RIM), manufacturer of the BlackBerry is a good example of a company that we think is trying to change its alpha. It has been more than five years since RIM made the decision to change its alpha strategy from R&D / technology to marketing. R&D / technology had been RIM's alpha strategy since RIM's founding in 1984. It will probably take another five years or more for RIM to complete the culture change from being a technology-driven firm to being a marketing-driven one.

RIM had a very difficult year in 2011. Product launches were late. The RIM network suffered some high profile global failures, leaving users with no service and wondering whether to switch to a competitor. The launch of its tablet product, the PlayBook, was problematic.

We don't think it is coincidence that RIM is now experiencing challenges that threaten its very survival.

RIM management was trying to convert the company culture from being technology-driven to being marketing-driven. In other words, RIM was trying to move marketing, which had been an influencer on the R&D / technology alpha, into the lead, alpha position. A consequence was that R&D / technology would move back into an influencer position. But the focus on marketing, as the new alpha, moved growth from being an enabler to being an influencer.

We think the RIM technology function could not come to grips with the high growth arising because of the increased focus on marketing. The quality of RIM's products and services and the product development process all suffered because of the new focus on marketing and not R&D / technology. All of this was new to the R&D / technology function, which for decades was alpha and focused on improved product technology and reliability.

As a result of the change in alpha to marketing, improved product quality and reliability were no longer the top priorities. Product launches and understanding what the market wants next became the priorities. As a result, mistakes were made.

The RIM marketing guys are, quite frankly, new to the company and are just learning how to market RIM's products. Compared to Apple, the gold standard in marketing technology and RIM's arch nemesis, RIM cannot seem to do anything right in 2012. But then, marketing has long been Apple's alpha strategy and culture. Technology is secondary to marketing at Apple. It is an influencer. Apple's marketing gift is making technology "cool" and "user-friendly". RIM is still making the transition from technology as alpha to marketing as alpha.

We will also be making the argument that it is inappropriate to change or replace the alpha without first understanding the current alpha and implications of the change. For example, a retailer will have marketing as its alpha. A bank, arguably, should always have financial management as its alpha. Pension funds and insurers should always have risk as their alpha.

We just discussed what a challenge it has been for RIM to morph from a technology alpha to a marketing alpha. It is just as challenging to change strategy within an established alpha. Look at the major North American department store retailers. Their alpha has always been marketing. But for generations, that marketing strategy focused on products, not customers. For generations, many department store retailers presumed that if they provided products, customers would come. The department store was nothing more than a giant showroom for consumer products.

Then competition and change appeared in the 1990s, in the form of the Internet, "big-box" specialty stores, and highly focused apparel retailers. Department stores had to makes changes within their (alpha) marketing strategy to make their marketing more customer rather than product driven. This is something almost as hard to do as replacing the alpha itself with another one of the eight.

Why is it so hard to change strategy? It's because changing strategy requires a change in the culture. Any change in strategy requires a change in behavior. Behavior is what characterizes culture. In other words, the department stores had to change the way they did and thought about things in order to implement the new strategy. Changing culture takes time and money. Many once great department stores disappeared because they couldn't make the change, or at least not fast enough.

Configuring The Alpha Strategies

To show attendees of my courses how to identify the configuration of The Alpha Strategies, I first break the class into small groups. I give each group a set of eight alpha fridge magnets. Each fridge magnet is one of the eight alphas. This allows the groups to stick the alphas to the blackboard and move them around during their discussions.

I ask the groups to identify a high profile organization that is familiar to everyone in the group and then to identify the alpha for that company. I advise that usually the identification process is one of elimination. For example "We know it's not risk or organization management or business definition or growth."

Once they have identified the alpha, I ask the groups to consider if they can determine how the remaining seven alphas are configured behind the alpha lead, using The Alpha Strategies' remaining categories of influencers, and enablers.

I give the groups three pieces of direction.

First is the broad definition for each of the eight strategies.

The second is that alpha sets the culture for the organization as a whole and therefore, the alpha strategy should be the one that seems most likely to have created that culture.

Third is that two or maybe three strategies will be influencers. The influencers are those strategies that seem to most influence or constrain the implementation of the alpha and the enablers. The remaining strategies will be enablers.

The groups usually take about twenty to thirty minutes to agree upon alpha for their chosen company. Invariably, they can reach consensus on the influencers, as well. The enablers then become the remaining strategies. The groups then present to the class their opinion of the configuration of The Alpha Strategies. The structure of the alpha model allows the groups to quickly come to preliminary opinions on the way strategy is organized.

The issue is not whether their answers are "right." My students realize that all they have done is to create a working model of their anecdotal understanding of strategy configuration within their chosen company. They accept that this working model would then have to be tested through further research. Yet the quality of their presentations and discussions equals what one might expect to hear in a boardroom. The groups are talking about each of the eight strategies in a powerful and highly communicative way.

What do the participants achieve by doing this exercise?

For one, they learn the power of visible thinking. Visible thinking is the conversion of thought into a picture that can be shared with the group. The Alpha Strategies printed as eight individual strategy cards enables visible thinking and an exchange of opinions and ideas on strategy and how it is configured.

The groups learn that they know more about strategy than they thought they did.

We believe very strongly that current approaches to discussing strategy actually inhibit discussion.

Current approaches use an intimidating vocabulary of synonyms for strategy that shut down discussion because so many of us get confused by the barrage of terms bandied about. The discussion quickly focuses on words for strategy, such as "vision", "mission", "purpose", "goals", "objectives", "strategy", and "tactics" instead of a focus on the activities such as "marketing", "finance", "service delivery", "risk", and so on, that were supposed to be the object of the discussion.

They learn that current strategy practices seldom involve a holistic discussion of all of the eight strategies or the configuration of those strategies.

They learn that assumed knowledge is the biggest flaw in current planning practices. In particular, they learn that it cannot be assumed that there is a common understanding of current strategy or how it is configured.

They learn that different strategies, as alpha, produce different cultures.

The assumption in most strategic planning practices is that planning must start with an understanding of the customer and markets and then the products and services being offered by the organization to those customers and markets. The alpha configuration exercise teaches the groups that the most important first step is to understand current strategy and how that strategy is configured. The practice of analyzing customers and markets against offered products and services is simply due diligence exercise on one, and only one of the eight strategies, namely, the marketing strategy. The same due diligence has to be conducted on all of the remaining seven. And then there needs to be agreement on how current strategy is configured. Current planning practices do not address this.

They learn that alpha can be any of the eight strategies, subject to the realities of certain industries and the constraints placed on public sector and not-for-profit organizations.

For example, within the private sector, the insurance industry demands that risk be the alpha. Within the public sector, the alpha is identified in the mandate of most public sector organizations, with risk being the alpha for all regulators, for example, and service delivery being the typical alpha for many other public sector organizations.

They learn to appreciate that one of the most significant impacts that a strategy decision can have is moving strategies from one position to another in the configuration. In particular, they learn the significance of trying to change the lead or alpha strategy. These impacts must be considered if there is to be properly informed decision making on issues of strategy.

But, most importantly, they learn how to present their own organization's strategic plan.

The Alpha Strategies represent the current strategic plan. The Alpha Strategies dynamic model enables them to identify and discuss the alpha. Then they can move to discussing the influencers and enablers.

Having presented the way strategy is being implemented today, they can then identify how factors in the external environment may be impacting the strategies of the model. And they now have a way to see how any proposed change to strategy to address those factors might impact the present configuration of strategy and the consequences arising from that change.

CHAPTER 3
ALPHA STRATEGIC PLANNING

Framing the Need to Understand Current Strategy

We think the starting point for strategic planning must be a review of the current eight strategies common to all organizations. Our assumption is "How can you consider a change in strategy if you do not understand current strategy?"

In this chapter, we are going to look at why this simple starting point is not typically used. We think this is because there is fundamental confusion about what a strategic plan is.

We are then going to show how The Alpha Strategies framework can be used to make sense of current strategy by looking at the strategic plans of three major, highly successful organizations, Stantec, Ford, and IBM.

The real power of The Alpha Strategies is in its ability to capture and present current strategy and strategy configuration of any organization. This is important to us because we see so many organizations that say they don't have a strategy or they don't have a plan. We show them how to use The Alpha Strategies framework to quickly document descriptions of their current strategies and to understand how those strategies are currently configured, including the identification of the alpha or dominant strategy.

These strategy descriptions and their configuration then form the basis for a much longer discussion either by board members or management or both on current strategy. As far as we are concerned, planning cannot begin until the hows and whys of current strategy are well understood by decision makers.

We are going to show how we apply The Alpha Strategies model by using some publicly traded companies. These companies make for good examples because they are required by securities laws to disclose a lot of information about their strategies. While this information is seldom organized into a single location as The Alpha Strategies, invariably, all of the alphas are addressed somewhere in the various disclosure materials.

Defining Strategic Planning

The fact is that there is no real consensus at this time on what constitutes a strategic plan. It seems that everyone believes they are doing "strategic planning" or "strategic business planning" or some such variant. Pull the words "strategic plan" apart and you are left with the term "strategic" which is the adjectival form of the noun, "strategy", and the word, "plan," which is synonymous with an arrangement. We have already defined strategy as being a choice of action. Quite literally, therefore, "strategic plan" can mean a plan of strategy or an arrangement of choices of action. What nonsense! It's no wonder there is confusion over the term.

On this basis, I guess you could say that anyone undertaking planning is preparing a strategic plan. This would be fine except that preparing a strategic plan is fundamentally different from all subsequent strategy planning in the organization. This is because the strategic plan is the only plan that sets direction and expectations for all further planning throughout the organization. That planning, whether it is called business planning, departmental planning, functional planning, project planning, or whatever, starts with looking to the strategic plan for guidance from the expectations created by it.

In the military world, a strategic plan is defined as a plan of war. This is not a helpful in the world of business management so we will ignore this definition although scores of business book authors and academics keep trying to relate military strategy to the body of knowledge called strategic management. It is hard for me to understand how strategies of destruction and killing have anything to do with business management.

When we look at the planning literature for for-profits, not-for-profits, and public sector organizations, there seems to be an unending selection of definitions for the term, strategic plan. The typical definitions seem to be framed in terms of content, process, or purpose.

A content focused definition might say something like: "*A strategic plan is a plan which addresses the values, vision, mission, and goals of the organization.*" A process focused definition of a strategic plan might look as follows: "*A strategic plan is a disciplined effort to produce fundamental decisions and actions that will guide the organization.*" The purpose focused definition might suggest: "*A strategic plan is one which will alter the look of an organization.*"

While we think all definitions should be content centric, the example given above of the content focused definition falls into the trap of reciting synonyms for strategy, thus rendering the definition useless. The process centric definition above fails to identify any process other than the process characteristics, namely, *a disciplined effort.* This is not helpful because all the definition is saying is that the strategic planning process takes effort. How is this helpful? Or was it assumed that other types of strategy planning do not take any effort? The example given of the purpose based definition is just plain wrong. A strategic plan should not regularly alter the way an organization looks. In the parlance of The Alpha Strategies, this would suggest that the strategic plan only focuses on changing the lead or dominant strategy, which is the one which sets the culture and, therefore, look of the organization.

Therefore, the assumption is that every strategic plan needs to focus on changing the alpha for the organization and, as a consequence of that, the culture of the organization. This is a deeply problematic assumption.

Our definition of strategic planning is content focused. We believe the strategic plan sets direction and expectations for all subsequent strategy planning and implementation throughout the organization by reviewing The Alpha Strategies for the organization as a whole, including their configuration, against changing external factors and stakeholder expectations to determine whether those strategies and their configuration are appropriate.

This definition places responsibility for approval and oversight of the strategic plan squarely on the shoulders of the board of directors, which is appropriate since one of the principal duties of the board is the approval and ongoing oversight of the strategic plan.

The definition also makes it clear that boards are responsible for eight strategies. Too often, boards seem to focus almost exclusively on the financial management strategy and financial performance metrics. The structure of The Alpha Strategies reminds us that there are seven other strategies that warrant just as much attention as financial management. It seems that the other seven strategies too often only get attention when there is a crisis.

The Alpha Strategies of Stantec

For our first example on how to use the model, we have chosen Stantec Inc., a firm listed on the Toronto and New York Stock Exchanges. We looked at the documents provided on the Stantec website, including the annual report, securities filings, and posts on the website to determine our opinion of the first draft of a description of each of the eight strategies.

The company website tells us that the Stantec vision is to grow to become a top ten global design firm. This tells us that the alpha is probably growth.

We will be making the point later on that we associate the term "vision" with the outcome of the long term pursuit of the alpha strategy. Therefore, when we see a vision statement, we assume it will identify the alpha.

We learn, from the security filings disclosures, that some fifteen years ago, Stantec was a small engineering services firm. We would guess that its alpha at that time, when it was an engineering consulting firm, was very probably service delivery because it had been in business for since the 1950s without any significant growth.

The decision was then made to replace service delivery, as alpha, with growth. No doubt, the board and management must have seen an opportunity to be a consolidator in North American engineering services industry and to grow by buying up other engineering firms. The company started more than fifteen years of acquisitions. In that time, Stantec grew to $1.2 billion in annual revenue with over 11,000 employees and offices all over the North America.

The growth strategy is stated on the website as: "To become and remain a top 10 global design firm." This is something which Stantec intends to achieve through a combination of acquisitions and internal growth, although clearly acquisitions have contributed more to date than internal growth. The implementation of the alpha, namely, growth, appears to be most constrained and influenced by three influencers, being business definition, risk, and financial management.

Stantec describes itself as offering professional consulting services in planning, engineering, architecture, interior design, landscape architecture, surveying, environmental sciences, project management, and project economics for infrastructure and facilities projects. This is the firm's business definition strategy. We think business definition is an influencer because it obviously has constrained and guided the growth strategy by containing growth to acquisitions within Stantec's chosen industry of professional engineering services.

The risk strategy is to focus on market, services, and life cycle diversification. This makes the risk strategy an influencer because it constrains and influences the acquisition strategy so that growth is focused on target purchases that maintain the diversification that the risk strategy requires.

Then there is the financial management strategy. We have paraphrased financial management as being "To source capital by being publicly-traded." As a public company, Stantec is under the constant scrutiny of the capital markets. The last thing Stantec wants is an acquisition that does not make sense to the markets because this is something that could damage its credibility and lower the value of its shares. The lower valuation would inhibit Stantec's ability to issue new equity at acceptable levels, among other things. The constraint that financial management imposes is that due diligence must be undertaken on each acquisition to assure that any acquisitions are going to be accretive very quickly.

The remaining strategies are the enablers, in our opinion. The enablers are marketing, organization management, R&D / technology, and service delivery. The marketing strategy is to be a top three service provider in chosen markets and to be seen as a single brand entity. The service delivery is described as having local strength, global expertise, one team, and infinite solutions. The organization management is described as using the balanced leadership model for top and bottom line focus. Finally, R&D / technology is clearly an enabler of productivity and is described as being for the support of the best trained, best informed, and best equipped employees.

The Alpha Strategies for Stantec can now be summarized on a single page and presented as follows:

Figure 12 The Alpha Strategies of Stantec

THE ALPHA STRATEGIES	STANTEC CONSULTING INC STRATEGIC PLAN
BUSINESS DEFINITION	TO FOCUS ON A FULL OFFERING OF PROFESSIONAL CONSULTING SERVICES FOR INFRASTRUCTURE AND FACILITIES PROJECTS IN NORTH AMERICA AND SELECTED INTERNATIONAL LOCATIONS
RISK	TO FOCUS ON MANAGING RISK THROUGH MARKET, SERVICES, AND LIFE CYCLE DIVERSIFICATION AND BY ASSUMING NO EXPOSURE TO COST OF CONSTRUCTION RISK
GROWTH	TO FOCUS ON BECOMING AND REMAINING A TOP 10 GLOBAL DESIGN FIRM WHICH IT WILL ACHIEVE THROUGH ACQUISITIONS AND INTERNAL GROWTH
FINANCIAL MANAGEMENT	TO SOURCE CAPITAL BY BEING PUBLICLY-TRADED AND TO FUEL GROWTH THROUGH ACQUISITIONS, AND TO MANAGE FINANCES IN COMPLIANCE WITH ALL REGULATORY REQUIREMENTS.
R+D / TECHNOLOGY	TO USE TECHNOLOGY TO ENABLE PRODUCTIVITY AND SUPPORT TO ACHIEVE THE BEST TRAINED, BEST INFORMED, AND BEST-EQUIPPED EMPLOYEES
ORGANIZATION MANAGEMENT	TO SOURCE PERSONNEL THROUGH ACQUISITIONS AND TO MANAGE THE ORGANIZATION USING A BALANCED LEADERSHIP MODEL OF MANAGING REVENUES AND EXPENSES
MARKETING	TO BE SEEN AS A TOP THREE SERVICE PROVIDER IN CHOSEN MARKETS AND TO BE SEEN AS A SINGLE BRAND ENTITY
SERVICE DELIVERY / PRODUCTION / MANUFACTURING	TO OFFER LOCAL STRENGTH, GLOBAL EXPERTISE; ONE TEAM; AND INFINITE SOLUTIONS IN ALL CHOSEN MARKETS

As far as we are concerned, this one page plan represents the starting place for the board and executive management to reach agreement on a description and common understanding of the strategic plan.

This one page document could be further supplemented with detail on each of the eight and would provide the board and management of any organization with the information required to assess recommendations on proposed changes to the strategies.

The additional detail could include process maps on the hows and whys of implementation of each of the strategies, the expectations and values driving and constraining their implementation, the external factors creating risks and opportunities that the strategies must address, the allocation of resources (financial, staffing, technology, etc.) required by each, and performance issues to date.

Based on our understanding of The Alpha Strategies for Stantec, we think the configuration of The Alpha Strategies at Stantec can be shown as follows:

Figure 13 Stantec Strategy Configuration

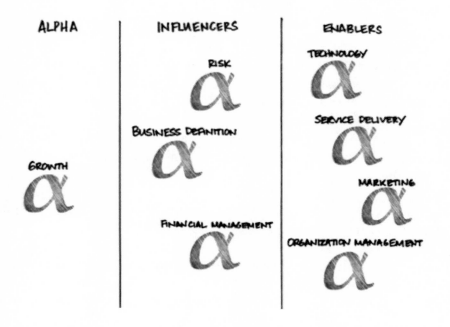

The configuration of The Alpha Strategies provides boards and management another means to understand strategy.

Instead of looking at strategies individually, it is possible to see how they relate to each other.

This, in turn, enables decision makers see the implications of proposed changes to strategy.

For example, while growth has been the dominant strategy or alpha at Stantec for more than fifteen years, a decision was made in early 2012 to start paying a dividend. One wonders whether that change to the financial management strategy has far greater implications for change to the other strategies.

The immediate question is "Can the growth strategy continue to be the alpha for Stantec if funds for acquisitions are now diverted to paying dividends?"

One of the consequences of the change to the Stantec financial management strategy might be that growth has to be replaced, as the alpha, with some other strategy, presumably service delivery, as the means to fuel the ongoing dividend payment obligation.

Up until now, service delivery has been an enabler. Service delivery would have to move from its enabling role to that of alpha if Stantec expects to generate the increased internal revenues and greater margins required to sustain the ongoing dividend payments.

This will be very challenging indeed because the culture at Stantec will need to change from being growth focused to being service delivery focused to achieve this strategy change.

There could also be changes to the influencers as growth moves back into an influencer role.

In any event, a change of alpha would certainly give rise to something in the order of a five to ten year implementation challenge for Stantec. Why so long? This is because Stantec must develop the behaviors associated with extraordinary service delivery if service delivery is to replace growth as the alpha.

This is not to say that Stantec has not been delivering excellent service in the past. However, the firm has been relying on acquisitions to fuel growth for over fifteen years. This means that the focus has been on adding companies to the Stantec stable, not driving more and more excellent service delivery.

The point is that the focus has not been on service delivery and as a result, the culture is not one of service delivery. The culture has been one of growth.

We would argue that the configuration visual above allows boards and management to see these issues more clearly and provides them with yet another tool to test proposals on strategy change and to understand the risks those changes face.

The Alpha Strategies of IBM

Our second example is no less than IBM, which celebrated its one hundredth anniversary in June 2011. This is no small feat in a world where companies come and go in a decade. IBM generates $100 billion a year in revenues and has over 425,000 employees worldwide.

Once again, we are going to use the eight strategy framework of The Alpha Strategies to build a description of the IBM strategic plan and a picture of IBM's strategy configuration.

IBM's website and its 2010 annual report and securities filings provide a wealth of information on the company. But let's start with how IBM describes its strategy on its web page titled "Our Strategy." The page contains a four paragraph summary titled, "IBM's Business Model." Our first reaction was, "So which is it, business model or strategy or strategic plan?"

Already we can feel those troublesome synonyms for strategy, doing their work to confuse and intimidate the reader. The strategy/business model page states that IBM focuses on high value, high growth segments of the IT industry. The first question that comes to my mind reading this is: "Are they describing their marketing strategy or their business definition strategy?"

Remember that my distinction between the two comes from Peter Drucker. Business definition answers the question: "What is my business?" Marketing, on the other hand, answers the question: "What products and services does the customer value?"

At first, this statement of focus looks like marketing. But because it describes segments rather than customers, it sounds more like how IBM wants to position itself within in the IT industry, which is the hallmark of business definition. That is how we arrived at the opinion that business definition is the alpha for IBM. A firm that uses business definition as its alpha strategy means that the company is constantly on the hunt to reposition itself. Consider what that might mean.

The Economist celebrated IBM's centennial with a two page story on the company in its January 2011 special annual edition of the newspaper. This is the issue in which *The Economist* makes predictions about what will happen in the coming year. *The Economist* described IBM as a "multinational nimble" and wondered whether the key to IBM's extraordinary success lay in its ability to reinvent itself continually, much the way pop artist Madonna seems to in order to stay relevant and popular.

This ability of the organization to reinvent itself is, for us, a characteristic of the use of business definition as the lead or alpha strategy.

As further support for our position, we note that IBM uses the words "shifts" and "transformation" a lot in its description of its strategy in its 2010 annual report. The words shift and transformation are quite different from words that would be typically used in a marketing strategy and focused on what customers think is value. However, these words, for us anyway, describe perfectly a company using business definition as the alpha.

As for its marketing strategy, IBM makes the following statement: "Helping clients succeed in delivering business value by becoming more innovative, efficient and competitive through the use of business insight and information technology (IT) solutions."

The firm's website strategy page talks about IBM's strategic investments in technology (R&D / technology) and its capabilities (service delivery).

And the page finishes by saying that the financial model (i.e., financial management) supports this business model.

Based on these descriptions of strategy, our opinion is that IBM's alpha strategy is business definition.

The influencers would seem to be service delivery, marketing, and R&D / technology simply because those are the strategies that are the most discussed in "Our Strategy."

IBM says that its financial management "supports" its business model presumably of business definition, as alpha, and marketing, service delivery, and R&D / technology as the influencers.

Based on the analysis of IBM's strategy page we would suggest The Alpha Strategies are organized as follows:

Figure 14 IBM Strategy Configuration

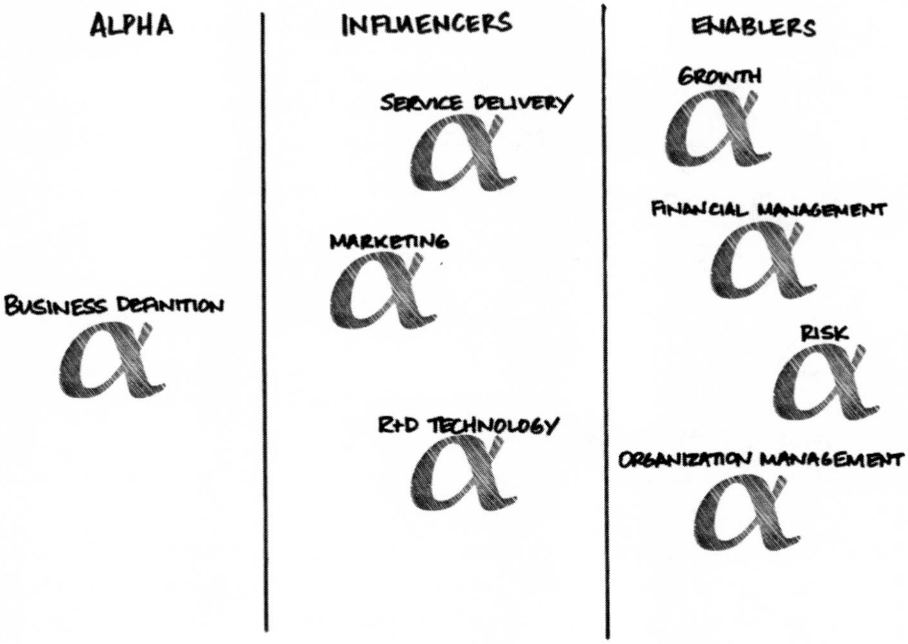

Our take on an overview of the IBM strategic plan, as seen through the lens of The Alpha Strategies, is as follows.

Figure 15 The Alpha Strategies of IBM

THE ALPHA STRATEGIES	IBM STRATEGIES
BUSINESS DEFINITION	CONTINUAL MOVEMENT TO FOCUS ON HIGH-VALUE, HIGH-GROWTH SEGMENTS OF IT
RISK	TO HAVE A THOUGHTFUL AND COMPREHENSIVE APPROACH TO CORPORATE CITIZENSHIP THAT IBM BELIEVES ALIGNS WITH IBM'S VALUES AND MAXIMIZES THE POSITIVE IMPACT OF WHICH IBM, AS A GLOBAL ENTERPRISE, IS CAPABLE
GROWTH	TO FOCUS ON HIGH-GROWTH SEGMENTS OF IT THROUGH ACQUISITIONS (116 OVER THE LAST 10 YEARS) AND INTERNAL GROWTH THROUGH INITIATIVES SUCH AS SMARTER PLANET AND GROWTH MARKETS
FINANCIAL MANAGEMENT	TO BE PUBLICLY TRADED ON THE NEW YORK AND CHICAGO STOCK EXCHANGES
R+D / TECHNOLOGY	TO FOCUS ON TRANSFORMATIONAL IT PRODUCTS AND SERVICES THROUGH PATENT LEADERSHIP (5,896 PATENTS IN 2010, 18TH STRAIGHT YEAR OF PATENT LEADERSHIP)
ORGANIZATION MANAGEMENT	TO DRIVE +8 BILLION IN PRODUCTIVITY IMPROVEMENT OVER THE NEXT 5 YEARS (2010-15)
MARKETING	TO OFFER SERVICES FOCUSING ON SERVICES, SOFTWARE, HARDWARE, FUNDAMENTAL RESEARCH, AND FINANCING
SERVICE DELIVERY / PRODUCTION / MANUFACTURING	TO DELIVER GLOBAL BUSINESS SERVICES, GLOBAL FINANCING, GLOBAL TECHNOLOGY SERVICES, AND SOFTWARE, SYSTEMS AND TECHNOLOGY

The business definition strategy, as we discussed above, is about continual focus on opportunities in emerging high value, high growth segments of the I.T. industry. This strategy has seen IBM exit older lines of business, such as personal computers, and move more and more into every aspect of services and software.

The risk strategy, as the annual report outlines it, has the focus we would expect on financial risks. But it is IBM's approach to corporate responsibility that, for me, best shows how it manages risk. The firm believes that if it acts in accordance with its values and beliefs as a responsible corporation, that approach will reduce its risks.

Growth for IBM will continue to come through acquisitions and through internal initiatives focusing on rapidly expanding, valuable opportunities, such as those it lists in its annual report ("Business Analytics and Optimization," "Cloud and Smarter Computing," and "Growth Markets"). IBM manages its finances by being a public company listed on the New York and Chicago stock exchanges and outside the United States.

IBM's R&D / technology is all about the research that results in patents. The IBM annual report notes that for eighteen consecutive years, IBM has filed more patents than any other company.

IBM bases its organization management on a culture of driving productivity. Marketing is about offering services in financing, fundamental research, hardware, and software. And IBM delivers services that fulfill its marketing promise of suites of services. These suites are organized into Global Business Services, Global Financing, Global Technology Services, and Software, Systems, and Technology.

The Alpha Strategies of Ford Motor Company

Our third example on how to use The Alpha Strategies framework to identify and present strategy is Ford Motor Company. Once again, we looked at its securities filings, including its annual report, website, and the description of its strategic plan contained in its 2010 annual report.

This is a great enterprise that survived a global financial meltdown without the need to seek bankruptcy protection or government bailouts to help it. That is why we picked Ford. The greatest challenge has to be taking something great and making it even better. For us, that challenge is exploring whether Ford could improve its strategy communications

Ford calls its strategic plan the One Ford Plan and provides a welcome amount of detail on it. It is described on the Ford website as having four components, being to:

- *aggressively restructure to operate profitably at the current demand and the changing model mix*
- *accelerate development of new products our customers want and value;*
- *finance our plan and improve our balance sheet; and*
- *work together effectively as one team, leveraging our global assets*

The first bullet would seem to be about production; the second, about marketing; the third, about financial management; and the fourth, about organization management. The document does not identify the alpha strategy, but we will assume the four bullets include alpha and its influencers.

Our first priority is to try to uncover alpha. You have to ask yourself, "Why do companies make it so hard to identify their dominant strategy?"

There are two obvious candidates in the One Ford Plan. Maybe marketing is one? Perhaps manufacturing? The reality is that with Ford's outsourcing of many of its requirements, manufacturing now means the very sophisticated assembly of components manufactured by its suppliers. So perhaps manufacturing is an influencer to marketing? Or is marketing an influencer to manufacturing?

As for influencers, financial management seems very important. Growth is not a high profile choice in the line-up of possible influencers. The One Team strategy, probably organization management, seems more important. That would make sense with the company's many employees. But one wonders where R&D / technology might fit in.

We can now go from a broad overview of Ford's strategy statements into more of the details of the One Ford plan on the website to see if we can identify the alpha and its influencers.

With that in mind, let's take a closer look at the text within bullet one above. Its title reads: "Aggressively Restructure to Operate Profitably." It contains six sub-bullets. These seem to involve at least three of the eight strategies of the alpha model: manufacturing, marketing, and organization management.

I say *at least* three because the text also mentions investment, arguably invoking financial management. There is also some detail on planned action in product development and that could mean R&D. Finally, a portion of the rationale behind brand and model consolidation could be about rethinking the business definition, being how Ford wants to position itself in the industry.

My point is that the first bullet of the One Ford Plan refers to at least three and maybe as many as six of the eight strategies of the alpha model. We think that is confusing.

The first sub-bullet within "Aggressively Restructure to Operate Profitably" is "Brands." It speaks to changes under way in the company's various brands, such as its discontinuing of the Mercury model and its sale of Aston-Martin, Jaguar, Land Rover, and Volvo.

This brand focus and brand mix clearly form part of Ford's marketing strategy. But then the sub-bullet point speaks to how Ford is reorganizing its manufacturing and assembly plants to address the demand for smaller, more fuel efficient vehicles in order to respond to global demand for them. All of a sudden, the plan is mixing and mashing manufacturing and marketing in the first sub-bullet.

The second sub-bullet is "Manufacturing." It speaks to Ford's manufacturing strategy, being to ensure adequate overseas production capability to meet demand in emerging markets. But it also mentions having assembly plants with flexible body shops, which may be referring to the R&D / technology strategy's impact on manufacturing. And then there is reference to the necessary investment. Is this about financial management? Once again, instead of addressing one strategy, titled, "Manufacturing," the paragraph addresses at least three strategies: manufacturing, R&D / technology, and financial management.

"Suppliers" is the third sub-bullet. Ford has a manufacturing plan to restructure and reorganize the global supply chain. The strategy is to transition to the use of a smaller number of suppliers with each supplier being expected to provide the total global volume of specific vehicle components required for the manufacturing process. This sub-bullet is addressing only manufacturing and, as a result, is quite clear in its messaging.

The fourth sub-bullet, "Ford and Lincoln Dealerships," is focused on the marketing strategy only and clearly addresses the plan to "right size" the dealership network. As a result, this bullet is clear in its messaging.

The fifth sub-bullet, "Product Development," sounds as though it might be addressing marketing but it also mentions using R&D / technology to engineer each global vehicle line and delves into aspects of manufacturing. As a result, it is not clear what strategies are being talked about.

"Ford Credit," the sixth and final sub-bullet, clearly outlines the organization management strategy, being a plan to reduce Ford Credit's worldwide staff by 1,000.

Of the six bullet points, only the third, "Suppliers," the fourth, "Ford and Lincoln Dealerships," and the sixth, "Ford Credit," are clear. That is because they each address one and only one strategy.

We gathered up the four big bullets in the One Ford Plan and then mapped them to The Alpha Strategies. We wanted to get a picture of way the various strategies in the One Ford Plan tie into The Alpha Strategies. Because, like you, the poor reader at this point, we felt we were up to our necks in a swamp.

The table we prepared below shows our analysis.

We listed the strategies of the alpha model down the left side column.

Across the top row appear the four points of the One Ford Plan in the 2010 annual report.

We went through the first point in the plan together in some detail above, noting when we thought other strategies were mentioned. We used the same approach to analyze the remaining three remaining points of the One Ford Plan on Ford's website and to complete our table.

Figure 16 One Ford Plan Mapping to The Alpha Strategies

THE ALPHA STRATEGIES	AGGRESSIVELY RESTRUCTURE TO OPERATE PROFITABLY	ACCELERATE DEVELOPMENT OF NEW PRODUCTS OUR CUSTOMERS WANT AND VALUE	FINANCE OUR PLAN AND STRENGTHEN OUR BALANCE SHEET	WORK TOGETHER EFFECTIVELY AS ONE TEAM
BUSINESS DEFINITION	X			
RISK		X		X
GROWTH	X			X
FINANCIAL MANAGEMENT	X	X	X	
R+D / TECHNOLOGY	X	X		
ORGANIZATION MANAGEMENT	X	X	X	X
MARKETING	X	X	X	
SERVICE DELIVERY / PRODUCTION / MANUFACTURING	X	X	X	

What does this analysis tell us? Well, the good news is that every one of the eight alpha strategies is addressed. The bad news is that the One Ford Plan tries to address multiple strategies at a time and this is very confusing.

We picked Ford to analyze because Ford is a great company doing a great job. We are not interested in criticizing. The real challenge is to take something good and make it better.

We think Ford could have structured its One Ford Plan around The Alpha Strategies and produced better strategy messaging.

The next table shows how we think the strategies of the One Ford Plan could be better organized based on The Alpha Strategies.

Figure 17 The Alpha Strategies of Ford

BUSINESS DEFINITION	"FOCUS ON THE CORE FORD BRAND"
RISK	"DRIVE QUALITY; DRIVE SAFE; DRIVE GREEN; DRIVE SMART"
GROWTH	"PURSUE GROWTH IN KEY EMERGING GLOBAL MARKETS TO BECOME A TRULY GLOBAL CAR COMPANY"
FINANCIAL MANAGEMENT	"FINANCE OUR PLAN AND STRENGTHEN OUR BALANCE SHEET"
R+D / TECHNOLOGY	"BUILD ON OUR NEW TECHNOLOGIES"
ORGANIZATION MANAGEMENT	"WORK TOGETHER EFFECTIVELY AS ONE TEAM"
MARKETING	"AGGRESSIVELY RESTRUCTURE TO OPERATE PROFITABLY"
SERVICE DELIVERY / PRODUCTION / MANUFACTURING	"ACCELERATE DEVELOPMENT OF NEW PRODUCTS OUR CUSTOMERS WANT AND VALUE"

While we think these are the basic strategies of the One Ford Plan, we still haven't identified the Ford alpha or its influencers and enablers.

As one of the largest automakers in the world, we are going to assume that manufacturing is the dominant strategy, or alpha, at Ford.

The influencers are marketing, financial management, and R&D / technology. We base this opinion on the emphasis given to these strategies in our reading of the One Ford Plan.

The enablers, by process of elimination, would therefore be organization management, risk, business definition, and growth.

We think the dynamic model of the Ford strategies is as follows:

Figure 18 Ford Strategy Configuration

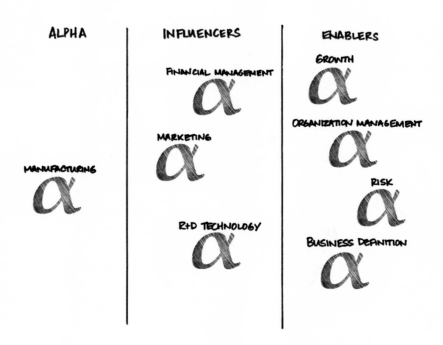

Manufacturing focuses on consolidation of the vendor supply chain production of global vehicle lines. Marketing addresses emerging global markets demand for smaller, fuel efficient vehicles, and brand consolidation. Financial management is all about strengthening the balance sheet and other financial issues. R&D / technology addresses the engineering hub strategy and technological advances.

The usefulness of The Alpha Strategies format is that it can present a focused description of each of the eight strategies. Once the audience understands what each of the eight is, then there can be a description on how the eight relate to and support each other. This description would start with the identification of the alpha strategy and its influencers. Then it would address the remaining strategies, the enablers.

The Message for Boards, Owners, and Senior Executives

Do you understand the eight strategies of your organization? Do you understand how those strategies are configured? Do you understand which of the eight is the alpha or dominant strategy leading your organization and setting its culture?

If the answer is "No." to any one of these questions, then your organization is at risk—the risk of flawed implementation or worse: replacing a perfectly good strategy with a bad one. This is what current strategic planning practices drive us to do!

Did you have trouble following our analysis of Stantec, Ford, and IBM? If you say "YES!", then you are beginning to understand what we are trying to say about present practices presenting and communicating strategy and the strategic plan. Those practices make understanding strategy almost impossible! The Alpha Strategies provides a framework to organize the multiple strategies that are evident in any organization.

How can we be so certain that understanding current strategy is the starting point for all strategic planning? Well, for one, I have yet to see a board that could agree on descriptions of current strategy. And I have been to a fair number of board meetings in my career.

Do you really think all the members of the Board of Ford Motor Company understood what the One Ford Plan was saying? I would suggest that you need to be a Philadelphia lawyer to work your way through the One Ford Plan. Using The Alpha Strategies framework allowed us the reframe the plan, but I would suggest that the reframing would only be the starting point of a much deeper discussion of the Ford strategies.

And even if you, as the CEO, or the chair of the board, or as a member of the executive management team or board itself, think you understand the strategies of the organization and how they are configured, then you have to ask yourself "I wonder if my fellow board members or management team members have the same understanding of these strategies as me?" You will quickly find that he answer is very likely going to be "No."

This was the question that McKinsey & Company set out to answer several years ago. McKinsey & Company is the world's leading strategy consulting firm and it surveyed the management and boards of more than a thousand companies around the world. The results can be found on the McKinsey website. McKinsey found that management generally believed a large member of its board members did not understand the long term strategies of the company. The same study found that board members believed the same thing about the management team. The McKinsey finding tells us that strategy communication and understanding is a big problem at the most senior level of more than a thousand organizations. If it is a problem at the top, how clear do you think the strategies are to the rest of the folks in the company—being the folks who are expected to implement strategy?

That's one of the drivers for writing this book and offering the model of The Alpha Strategies. We want to produce a better way to understand, discuss, and communicate strategy. We are not satisfied that boards and management are talking about the right things in the right way and, as a result their decisions on strategy are not well-informed, compromising the chances of successful implementation of strategy.

As we said in our introduction to the book, we believe the subject of strategy and its planning has been wrapped in mysterious processes and an intimidating vocabulary of synonyms and buzz words for too long. Forget those processes and the buzz words. Focus on filling in The Alpha Strategies framework with the actual strategies of the organization. And then, when there is consensus that the strategies are described accurately (i.e the descriptions are consistent with what is actually being implemented), the focus can turn to agreeing on the alpha strategy and how the remaining strategies are configured into influencers and enablers behind that alpha.

Our sincere hope is that The Alpha Strategies framework makes the subject more accessible and enables board members and management to start having meaning discussions on current strategy, the starting point for understanding any proposed change to strategy.

CHAPTER 4
ALPHA BUSINESS PLANNING

Expectations Drive All Business Planning

We have focused on the use of The Alpha Strategies for strategic planning. Now we need to turn our attention to its implications for business planning, the means of strategy implementation.

Most books on strategy would have us believe that strategy development comes from "out-of-the-box" thinking and creativity. The reality is very different. All strategy implementation is driven by expectations created and imposed by the strategic plan on all subsequent strategy development.

If those imposed expectations are clearly articulated, then strategy implementation can take its direction from those expectations and stays aligned with the intent of the strategic plan.

Therefore, we think business plan strategy development is founded on identification and prioritization of expectations imposed on the business planner.

Once the expectations have been identified and prioritized, then the business planner can test the most important expectations (imposed priorities) against the business planner's external reality. In this way, the imposed expectations inform the business planner on what the priorities are to be and the external reality check allows development of strategy consistent with and tailored to that reality.

The difference between strategic planning and business planning is that strategic planning starts with an agreed description of current strategy and its configuration and then reviews those strategies against a changing external reality to determine if those strategies and the configuration of them are still appropriate.

Business planning (indeed, all strategy implementation planning, including project planning) starts with an understanding and prioritization of the expectations imposed on the business planner by the strategic plan.

As with other words in the planning lexicon, we find the term "business planning" to be terribly unhelpful. In plain English, the term would be "planning for the business."

No wonder, when I am teaching, I get asked, "What is a business plan?" more times than any other question. My answer is that business planning means all planning required for implementation of the intent of the strategic plan. As far as I am concerned, business planning includes business unit, departmental, functional, divisional, subsidiary, project planning, and any other names that an organization might use for strategy implementation planning.

Another reason I think so many of us struggle with strategic planning and business planning practices is that so many academics and so-called experts would have us believe that strategic thinking is the same as problem solving. Strategic thinking and problem solving are two distinct subsets of critical thinking. They are not the same. Problem solving is not appropriate for strategy issues.

Consider that Drucker observed, in *The Practice of Management* (1954), that strategic decisions are not problems to be solved.

Let's look at the characteristics of strategic thinking from a manager's perspective. The question is "What do managers think about when they are thinking about strategy?" Ask any manager this question and the off-the-cuff answer will likely be something like, "Whatever I have to do to keep my boss happy!"

What managers are really doing is thinking about how to meet the expectations imposed on them by their boss. What is the source of the boss's expectations? Hopefully it is the strategic plan of the organization as a whole. That is the only way implementation strategies throughout the organization will stay aligned with the intent of the strategic plan. The tools a manager has to satisfy these imposed expectations are the responsibilities assigned to the manager (i.e., his job description).

All of this supports our definition of strategic thinking as managing assigned responsibilities in such a way as to meet imposed performance expectations. With this definition, it is possible to understand that everyone, from the chief executive officer to individual employees, must be thinking strategically.

To show how strategic thinking works down through an organization, I offer this story.

A Canadian call center manager was ordered by his American boss to implement a sixty-hour work week. The CEO had sent all employees an e-mail saying, "to address the difficult business conditions facing us, I think we need to institute a sixty hour work week." This email went on to invite anyone who had an objection to respond directly to the CEO. It is not known whether anyone responded.

After checking the realities of the law on hours of work per week, being a factor outside the control of the manager, the Canadian call center manager had to call the boss to inform him on Canadian labor laws, including the conditions triggering the requirement to pay overtime.

The boss was shocked, but rather than pay overtime on the difference between sixty hours a week and the requirements under the law, the boss elected to leave things as they were in Canada. The boss knew that the CEO would not expect to pay more for the increased hours.

In this example, you can see how the expectation imposed on the manager is likely only to be modified by uncontrollable factors in the manager's external environment. In this case the expectation was modified because it was not consistent with labor laws.

On another note, this is an excellent example of how the business plan can push back on the strategic plan. This is hardly bottom-up planning. It is simply supplying additional information to decision makers before implementing action to achieve the imposed expectation. The strategic plan is developed from a high level assessment of external factors. Many times, the high level assumptions about the external factors are at odds with the external reality a business planner must address.

Now, let's look at problem solving.

In problem solving, the first challenge is to identify the problem. There are no specific expectations to guide identification of the issue. There could be an infinite number of possible descriptions of the problem, depending on who is conducting the analysis and how that analysis is conducted.

Having identified the problem, the next step is identifying a solution. Once again, there could be an infinite number of solutions.

Consider this story about problem solving.

It is the early fall of a new school year. A harried high school principal has finally identified why the mirrors in the girls' washrooms are constantly being stained with lipstick, creating a significant cleaning challenge for the unionized custodial staff, which in turn was causing grumbling about grievances and work stoppages.

At first, the principal thought the cause might be graffiti or vandalism. After some investigation, she identified that the cause was the result of a new fad called lip blotting. The young girls were using the mirrors, rather than Kleenex, to blot their freshly applied lipstick in order to achieve the desired fashion look of the moment.

After worrying for days about how to solve the problem, an answer came to our hardworking principal as she lay in bed thinking about the situation in the middle of the night. She fell soundly asleep, confident in the solution she had identified.

The next morning, she addressed the school at its morning assembly. Our intrepid principal advised the assembled students that she wished to inform the young ladies in the audience on changes the custodial staff had made to their cleaning procedures in order to address the lipstick stained mirrors.

She advised the young ladies that, to save time, the janitors were dipping their cleaning brushes in the toilets to first wet the brush and then they were wiping down the mirrors with the wet brush to remove the stains.

A look of horror quickly appeared on the girls' faces. After the principal's explanation, the girls no longer used the mirrors to blot their lips. Problem solved.

The difference between strategic thinking and problem solving is that in the strategic thinking story, the call center manager could chose to follow the boss's direction or not follow it. But if the choice was not to follow the boss's direction, the manager needed to provide a good explanation, which he did. The labor laws in his jurisdiction provided the complete explanation.

In the problem solving example, our high school principal could have chosen any number of solutions, all of which would have likely worked.

I point out to my students that if I assigned them both the call center story above and the high school principal problem without revealing how the stories end, they would all come back with the same answer to the call center manager's dilemma.

But as for the lip blotting problem, all of the groups would likely come back with very different acceptable, proposed solutions.

Problem solving involves finding an answer to a question when both the understanding of the question and, therefore, the proposed answer to it are equally suspect.

Strategic thinking involves identifying and using imposed performance expectations to provide direction to the way a manager should manage assigned activities.

Both are sub-sets of critical thinking, being the process by which an informed decision is made. Both are important skills in the workplace. But treating strategy as a problem to be solved is inappropriate because it will lead to a flawed conclusion.

The Role of the Board

Business plan strategy identification is dependent on clear communication of the expectations for implementation of the strategies of the strategic plan. It is the responsibility of the board to approve the strategies contained in the strategic plan, the expectations to guide implementation, and to understand generally how those strategies are being implemented.

This last point addresses the fact that not only is it a primary responsibility of the board to review and approve the strategic plan, the board is also responsible for the oversight of its implementation. This implementation is achieved through business plans. That is why boards need to understand business plans and the expectations required to guide their preparation so that acceptable strategies are proposed.

It is no wonder that many folks, me included, do not think it is possible for anyone to serve on multiple boards, particularly if the organizations are of any significant size.

How is it possible to have the time to learn and to understand how strategy is being implemented in multiple organizations, let alone address making informed decisions on changes to strategy?

The strategic plan is the only plan in the organization with the authority to set strategy direction and strategy implementation expectations for the organization as a whole. The role of the board of a for-profit, not-for-profit, or public sector corporation is to receive and review management's review of the strategic plan strategies against changing stakeholder expectations and factors in the external environment.

That review includes determining whether the choice of alpha, influencers, and enablers as well as the choice of strategies for each remains appropriate, given the external reality.

We use the term "review" because there will be very few circumstances where the strategies of the strategic plan aren't already up and running in an established organization, even if the strategic plan is not documented.

The role of the board is to understand what those current strategies are and generally how they are being implemented, and the factors that are impacting their performance.

To quickly illustrate the issues inherent in a strategy decision, let's look at what the Stantec board might have considered in making its decision to introduce a dividend. Strategy decisions are also known as "strategic issues". Let's first tackle a definition of that term.

"Strategic" is an adjective, meaning "concerned with strategy." We have already defined strategy as being a description of a chosen course of action. The second word, "issue", is a synonym for the word "question".

The common sense definition would have a strategic issue be a question of strategy. That logic begs the question "What questions are there about strategy?"

The most basic question is "Should we improve the execution of existing strategy or should we replace existing strategy with a new strategy?"

This, for us, becomes the definition of strategic issue. It is a question of strategy with the question being whether to improve existing strategy or to replace it.

Let's return to the Stantec strategic issue. Stantec Inc., a North American, publicly traded, professional services firm, has pursued growth as its alpha for more than a decade. In February 2012, the company announced that it would start paying a dividend for the first time in its history.

We would hope that this decision came as a result of the board's review of the strategic plan and the external factors impacting that plan. From this review obviously came a conclusion that a change to the financial management strategy change was necessary, presumably to address shareholder demand for value creation in the current low interest rate environment. That change was to introduce a dividend. As such, the strategic issue clearly involved a change to existing strategy.

But with the introduction of this change, it looks as though the board may have also made the bigger decision the replace growth as the alpha of the company with service delivery.

This seems to be signaled in the reality that returning funds to shareholders via a dividend rather than using that money to fuel growth is tantamount to saying that service delivery represents a better opportunity for growth than making acquisitions.

Or to put the point the way Peter Drucker would have said it, "Growth should be a consequence of good service delivery that makes customers want to return for more."

I would certainly hope the decision by Stantec to institute a dividend was not made as an isolated approval of a financial matter. I hope it was made with the realization that one of the consequences will likely be the need to change the alpha of the company from growth to service delivery and that this change could take ten years to affect.

If this implication was not understood, then performance could suffer because of the confusion which results from not understanding the strategy priorities. Is growth the priority or is it service delivery?

It is imperative that the board understand the full implications of any strategy before approving it, particularly, if it involves a change as significant as changing the alpha strategy.

The change also raises expectations for the operating business units to produce more internal growth, something that is bound to change the way the business units do business. Why? The simple answer is that the business units have been able to rely on acquisitions as the source of growth. Now that has been taken away.

Let's look at another story on board strategy approvals and identifying what the board should consider before making a decision.

This time the story involves an airline.

A passenger jet en route from Paris to Rio crashed into the Atlantic in 2009 killing all 228 people on board. The ensuing investigation determined that the flight crew consisted of a pilot and two co-pilots. The pilot was trained and sufficiently experienced to fly the plane. The copilots did not know how to fly the plane except when it was on autopilot and required very little input from the crew.

It must have been decided at that airline that the new generation of fully automated aircraft no longer required a full complement of experienced pilots who actually knew how to fly the plane. As a result, there would be just one experienced and qualified pilot flying the plane. The two copilots would be there to support the needs of the pilot.

Unfortunately, on the night of the crash, the pilot, being the one person on board capable of flying the plane, had left the cockpit to get some rest. As a result, he was not in the cockpit at the time the flight ran into difficulty. The subsequent investigation revealed that everything the copilots had done to manage the situation was wrong because they had no idea what to do. The plane crashed and everyone was killed.

I would like to think the decision not to use trained pilots was debated at length at a board meeting of that airline company although I have no way of knowing this and I have my doubts as to whether the issue was ever raised.

I would like to think that board members were informed on and fully understood all the differences between the old strategy, which required trained pilots, and the new strategy, which decided trained pilots were not necessary.

I truly believe that the cause of this horrific accident can be tracked directly to a decision on strategy. I only hope that it was an informed decision. I am not comfortable believing it was, based solely on my experience from having attended some many hundred board meetings.

I can hear the outcry from some readers. "Are we, as board members, expected to get into that level of detail?" Or from the management's side,

"Are we, as management, supposed to take that level of detail to the board?" The answer is yes.

Unfortunately, I have a feeling that the aircraft matter was likely presented as a recommendation for the purchase or leasing or financing of a new fleet of aircraft, when, in fact, the proposed transaction represented more than just a financial management strategy.

The change actually represented a fundamental change in the airline's service delivery strategy. In addition to service delivery, the impact on the risk, organization management, and technology strategies should have been addressed as well as the obvious financial management issue.

When folks die because of a decision to use untrained pilots, this tells me that the board's responsibility for informed decision making needs to involve going way beyond simply approval of the financing of bunch of airplanes.

The Role of Imposed Expectations

Each of the strategies of the strategic plan will be implemented through a further round of planning which is known most commonly as business planning. The expectations of the strategic plan are the principal driver of this strategy implementation.

This is how implementation plans stay aligned with the intent of the strategic plan. This is why management needs to understand and to know how to identify and to communicate the expectations set by the strategic plan.

The term, expectations, is wonderful because it is so well understood within organizations. After all, most individual performance is measured against achieving expectations. Why shouldn't we be also using the term to understand better how to develop and communicate strategy?

We broadly define expectations as "a hoped for outcome."

The expectations imposed on managers become their objectives for the coming year. This is an extraordinarily simple concept that is not well understood or even talked about, in our opinion. We still see business professors and facilitators telling their students and executive education classes to look to their job descriptions for the source of their coming year's objectives. This is just plain wrong. The job description speaks to the responsibilities they have been assigned. These responsibilities are to be managed consistently with the expectations imposed on them. Expectations are the source of objectives.

Other experts preach that the way to identify objectives for the coming year is to identify the problems that need to be solved. This approach confuses problem solving, which strategy implementation is not, with strategic thinking.

Even more disturbing is that the approach completely ignores the ongoing expectations; being the requirement to continue working on certain issues. When you think about it, the ongoing expectations, being those matters identified as business as usual, far outnumber the new expectations; being the expectation to begin some new initiative or change.

My visual for depicting the relationship of the strategic plans to all other planning in the organization is as follows:

Figure 19 Relationship of Strategic Plan to Business Plans

In the graphic above, we can see the large alphas of the strategic plan surrounded by the smaller alphas of business planning. We can see the dominant strategy of the organization as a whole, being the large lead alpha, followed by three large influencers and four large enablers. All of the large alphas are shown to be implemented through the smaller alphas.

While strategic planning starts with a review of the performance of each of The Alpha Strategies against changing factors in the external environment, business planning is supposed to start with an assessment of the expectations for strategy implementation imposed on the business planner, usually by the planner's boss.

The expectations of the boss are supposed to be consistent with the strategic plan. They are not always so. Many of us have worked for a boss who did not agree with the strategic plan and imposed expectations on us that we knew were at odds with the strategic plan. It didn't matter what we thought. What our boss wants is what keeps us in our job.

The reality is that expectations flow one way, from the top down. There is no such thing as bottom-up planning. Bottom-up planning is simply an information gathering process that supports strategy development and clarifies top-down imposed expectations for strategy implementation.

This difference between the starting point for strategic planning and for business planning is not an academic distinction. Let me tell a story to illustrate this point.

I was called into a large organization. The management team had completed a strategic planning and visioning process. Management now wanted to undertake business planning to implement the vision.

The team had come up with a vision statement something like, "We will be the world's finest producer of widgets." The team had also produced a slogan celebrating the employees of the firm. It was something like: "Our employees are our strength."

In my first meeting with the general manager, it became clear to me that, notwithstanding the size of the organization, that it was a Canadian subsidiary of an American parent company. The subsidiary was not preparing the strategic plan for the organization as a whole. It took direction from the American parent by way of the expectations imposed on it by the parent.

In other words, the subsidiary should not be undertaking strategic planning and looking to the external environment first. The general manager should have started by carefully identifying and analyzing the expectations imposed on him by his boss and the strategic plan of the parent company.

Unfortunately, that didn't happen. There is just too much confusion on how to plan and on the source of strategy. To show how far offside the subsidiary had gone by not understanding the difference between strategic and business planning; let's look at what happened when the strategic planning process was applied instead of the business planning process.

The general manager had called in a strategic planning facilitator. The facilitator began the planning process by having the management team scan the external environment for opportunities and threats, as though a strategic plan was being undertaken.

The team identified a huge opportunity in the Canadian marketplace for the widgets that the plant produced. It didn't take long for everyone on the team to get really excited about the prospects for the subsidiary. It seemed natural to embed this thinking into a vision statement. Thus was born the vision, "We will be Canada's first choice for widgets."

No doubt working on the enthusiasm and sense of accomplishment of the moment, the facilitator pointed out the need for the management team to recognize the folks who would be making it all happen, namely, the three hundred or so line workers producing the widgets. This result quickly followed: "Our employees are our greatest strength."

Of course, this sort of stuff tends to build on itself. Next, someone, maybe even the facilitator, is suggesting that the vision and the employee slogan should be printed on oversized banners so that they could be hung on the walls throughout the facility.

It was shortly after the posters were put up on the walls that I arrived at the plant for my first meeting with the general manager.

Going back to what happened at that first meeting between me and the GM, it became apparent to me very quickly that the general manager needed first to understand the expectations imposed on him and his subsidiary. These expectations come from the strategic plan of the American parent, as channeled through direction given to him by his boss.

To do this, we started by identifying and talking through each of The Alpha Strategies of the American parent. I explained that if we were to identify the expectations created by each of the strategies, then it was important to understand those strategies.

It came as no surprise to me that the alpha for the parent was production. The parent and all of the subsidiaries were manufacturers.

We identified the influencers as being financial management, technology, and marketing. Financial management was evident in the parent's keen focus on financial matters. Costs, margins, and tax structures were a part of every decision made in the organization, including the decision on where subsidiaries would be located outside of the United States.

Technology was identified as an influencer because of the extraordinary use of technology, particularly robotics, to enable the parent's highly productive manufacturing processes. Marketing was identified as an influencer because of the global recognition of the parent brand and product line. The remaining alpha strategies were identified as enablers.

Once we had documented those strategies, then we were ready to identify the expectations created by them. The mistake that had been made with the so-called strategic planning and visioning approach was not recognizing these expectations as the starting place for business planning.

A business planner who looks first to the external environment without understanding the expectations imposed on him or her by the strategic plan is unlikely to develop strategy that is aligned with the expectations of the strategic plan. There are just too many opportunities and threats to consider in the external environment without taking guidance first from the expectations in the strategic plan.

Having identified the strategic plan of the parent, we quickly identified three or four expectations created by The Alpha Strategies. In the course of identifying those expectations there were some surprises. These were announced by audible groans from the general manager. "How could I forget that?" was his comment after identifying the expectations created by the production strategy.

The parent company expected the Canadian subsidiary to produce whatever the parent directed it to produce. Over the last several years, that direction had been to produce widgets. But the subsidiary had no control over what the edict from the parent might be for the coming year. The parent had no particular interest in the Canadian market or what the subsidiary could do in that market if it was a standalone company. To the parent, the subsidiary was supposed to be simply a production source filling product orders from the parent.

This revelation, by itself, was fatal to the vision statement "to be Canada's first choice for widgets." The general manager knew it. That's why he had groaned.

The next groan came with the identification of expectations on organization management and technology. To summarize, the parent would not tolerate any union presence in its plants. As if that wasn't enough, to ensure maximum productivity and to mitigate the risk of unionization, the parent had developed a technology strategy focused on replacing workers with robotics.

I asked the general manager what this strategy, when implemented, might mean in terms of workforce numbers. He told me that virtually all of the line workers would become redundant once the robots were installed. So much for the employee slogan, "Our employees are our strength."

Our first conclusion, when the GM and I identified the expectations created by the parent company strategic plan, as interpreted and supplemented by the GM's understanding of the expectations of his boss, was that the vision statement and employee slogan were completely delusional.

The vision statement and employee slogan were founded on what the management team wanted to do rather than what the management team was expected to do. Now the GM's problem was how quickly to bring down the posters. In fairness, the GM and his team had been led astray by a so-called planning expert but that was small comfort to the GM.

This situation arose because of what I call "inside-out" thinking. The thinking is all centered on "What do we want to do?" It is a recipe for disaster because the choices of action (i.e., strategy) are infinite and not guided by the strategic plan.

Strategy is all about "outside-in" thinking. The choices of strategy are made obvious by considering the factors over which there is no control.

By far the most important external factor in all planning subsequent to the strategic plan is the expectations created by the strategic plan. Without these expectations setting direction and guiding subsequent strategy implementation, there would be a significant misalignment between the intent of the strategic plan and business plans.

Aligning Imposed Expectations with External Reality

We have made the case that business planning priorities are set by reference to the expectations and priorities imposed on business planners. The next step is aligning those expectations with external reality. All strategy is set by reference to external reality.

The GM in our previous example didn't have a hope in identifying the external factors that would be crucial to achieving the expectations imposed on him.

The difficulty the poor GM at the production facility caused for himself in the previous example was his failure to use imposed expectations to guide setting priorities for his business plan. It is these priorities that enable appropriate external factor identification.

The priorities the GM should have identified were to meet production quotas within prescribed cost and quality parameters. These priorities represented the most important expectations he was expected to achieve. This is what he was expected to do. Strategy identification should then have consisted of identifying the best ways to achieve those expectations.

Instead, he had been led to believe, by ignoring the strategic plan and its expectations, that he should be looking first at the external reality. It is easy to understand why he was misled. He was following the methodology for strategy planning that is recommended by most by business textbooks and authors. The reality is all strategy planning following strategic planning starts with understanding the expectations and priorities of the strategic plan.

The GM's mistake led to the flawed vision, "To be Canada's first choice for widgets." The GM had scanned the external environment and found the market for widgets in Canada to be the most attractive possibility. It would then become obvious that the marketing strategy would be the strategy most suited to addressing that external factor of markets and customers. But he could not have been more misguided or delusional, and he probably would have been fired if he had brought that business plan to his boss.

The priorities of the parent strategic plan clearly wanted the GM focused on more and more productive manufacturing.

The parent didn't care about market opportunities in Canada.

The external factors that seem most relevant to achieving the parent manufacturing expectation are going to be something like the cost inputs for labor, input components of the product itself, the production processes being used and maybe technology.

I say maybe technology because it is likely that the parent has already addressed the technology factor through its decision to deploy robotics throughout its production facilities.

With these external factors and realities identified, the GM could then begin to identify the strategies most appropriate to deliver to the expectations.

This is how strategy is identified. This is what is meant by, "Tell your people what you want and then leave them alone. Let them figure it out."

Strategic thinking means using imposed expectations to guide how assigned responsibilities are to be managed.

Strategy implementation in all organizations is the top-down communication of expectations.

If you tell your employees what you want, in a clear and compelling manner (which means giving them convincing rationale for the expectation), invariably, they will put their heads together and figure out how to deliver to that expectation.

The final point to be made in strategy identification is that new strategies are infinitely more challenging to put into place than improving existing strategy.

To demonstrate this, we are next going to consider why new strategy is so much harder to implement than existing strategy.

Consider the simple 2x2 matrix in the figure below.

Figure 20 Strategy Choices Matrix

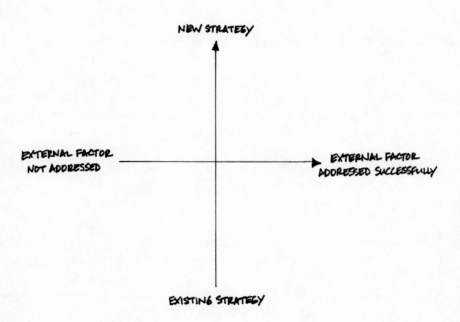

The vertical axis has "existing strategy" at the bottom and "new strategy" at the top. The horizontal axis runs from "External Factor Not Addressed"

on the left to "External Factor Addressed" on the right. This is the classic strategic thinking matrix, pitting what the manager controls, being strategy, against what cannot be controlled, being external factors.

All strategy implementation begins in the bottom-left quadrant because that is the quadrant in which the relevant external factor that needs to be addressed has been identified. And there is already an existing strategy which, on the face of it, does not appear to be addressing the factor.

A manager knows that staying in the lower left quadrant is not an option because the strategy is not addressing the external factor. The manager must decide whether to implement a new strategy first, (i.e., move to the upper left hand quadrant) as the means for addressing the external factor. Or as an alternative, the manager could work on improving the existing strategy before introducing any new strategy (i.e., move to the lower right hand quadrant).

The risks inherent in new strategy versus existing strategy implementation can be shown using the Cartesian plane depicted as:

Figure 21 Risks in New Strategy

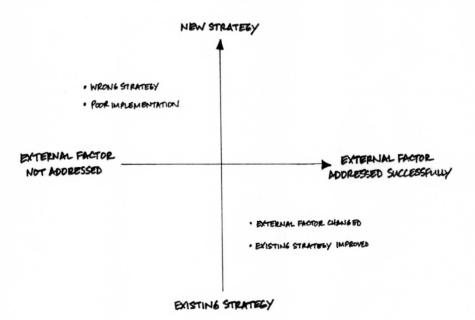

In the lower right hand quadrant, the external factor has been successfully addressed even though the existing strategy is still in place. What has happened? Maybe the external factor changed, making it no longer an issue to be addressed. Or perhaps all that was required were improvements to the existing strategy. Or maybe some other strategy addressed the factor.

The lesson to be learned is not to be too quick changing strategy. It is easier to improve existing strategy than it is to replace it with a new one. To see the proof of this, let's look at what happens when new strategy is implemented to address the external factor. When that happens, we move immediately into the upper left hand quadrant.

In the upper left hand quadrant, the new strategy is in place but the external factor has still not been addressed. How did this happen? There are three possible explanations. One is that the new strategy is the wrong strategy. The second is that poor implementation is the issue. The third is that the new strategy has not been allowed enough time to address the external factor.

For me, the upper left hand quadrant is the all-or-nothing quadrant. I think of Carly Fiorina, the CEO of Hewlett-Packard, who engineered the merger of HP with Compaq in 2002. The merger itself constituted her new strategy to address the threat to HP from increasing industry competitiveness.

Unfortunately, her strategy came under immediate and constant attack from certain shareholders of HP. Ms. Fiorina managed to secure approvals for the merger; however, no merger, particularly of that size, is going to deliver immediate results. She was finally forced out of the company in 2005 because the merger was seen as a failure, although, shortly thereafter, the benefits of the merger became clear.

The external factor Fiorina was trying to address was the threat of industry competiveness. She had hoped that by combining the company with Compaq, she could address both cost and breadth of product line issues that were at the heart of the lack of HP's competitiveness.

In the end, she was pushed out the door before it became obvious that her strategy was the exactly right one for the company.

The lesson is clear, as far as we are concerned.

If you choose to implement new strategy, do not underestimate the challenge. You are changing the way people have been taught to behave and that takes time and will face resistance.

CHAPTER 5
ALPHA VISION AND MISSION

The Alpha Definition of Vision and Mission

For us, a vision statement reflects the long term likely outcome from pursuit of the alpha strategy as guided by one or more of its influencers.

Well written vision statements, in our opinion, identify the alpha strategy and refer to one or more of the influencers. The alpha strategy is the dominant strategy. The influencers are the strategies that most influence and constrain the implementation of the alpha.

As for mission statements, we believe they should be "pure Drucker" and answer the question "What is our business?"

This means that the mission statement should say nothing beyond a description of how the organization is positioned in the competitive environment. This practice relegates the mission statement to its proper place as a description of the business definition / mandate strategy.

Many of the large publicly traded corporations are now treating the mission statement as a description of their business definition strategy. They have moved beyond the era of the vision and mission statements that attracted the attention of satirists such as Scott Adams and his Dilbert cartoons.

No doubt the advent of more stringent securities laws that have come into effect in the last decade have probably tempered many vision and mission statements, requiring them to be much more cautious when making forward-looking statements.

We think we see confirmation of this observation in Bain & Company's survey for 2011, available on the Bain website. Bain is one of the world's preeminent strategy consulting firms. The survey, an annual exercise by the firm since 1993, shows mission and vision statements, as a management tool, falling in popularity from first place in 1993 to third in 2011.

I suspect this finding would contrast sharply with a survey of smaller and medium sized businesses, not-for-profits, and entities in the public sector. These organizations seem to still fully embrace the flawed model of vision and mission statements abandoned by most publicly traded companies.

Stantec offers an example of a publicly traded firm with a vision statement consistent with our definition being the outcome of long term pursuit of the alpha. Its vision statement is: "to become and remain a top 10 global design firm." These words reflect the company's alpha strategy, being growth, as well as the role of the business definition as an influencer in guiding that long term outcome to occur within the design industry.

Stantec, like many organizations, offers no mission statement labeled as such. Instead it describes itself as follows: "Stantec, founded in 1954, provides professional consulting services in planning, engineering, architecture, interior design, landscape architecture, surveying, environmental sciences, project management, and project economics for infrastructure and facilities projects." This is clearly a description of the firm's business definition strategy.

Like many large organizations these days, General Electric (GE) does not have a vision statement. But then, I don't ever recall GE having a vision or mission statement. Imagine that! One of the largest, most successful businesses in the world has no vision statement! How can that be?

The simple answer is that GE understands strategy, communicates it well, and likely believes that a vision statement or a summation of the likely outcome of its long term pursuit of its alpha strategy would add no further value to its strategy communications.

For years, under the stewardship of Jack Welch, the GE website listed an answer, under the heading FAQs, to the question: "What is GE's mission statement?"

The answer was to the effect that GE does not have a mission statement and that the board of directors reviews GE's objectives annually.

Home Depot does not provide a vision or mission statement. Neither does Goldman Sachs. The vision of Raytheon Corporation, the big weapons company, is "to be the most admired defense and aerospace company through our world-class people and technology." This suggests that manufacturing leads, with organization management ("its people") and R&D / technology being the influencers of the manufacturing alpha.

The benchmark for poor vision and mission statements may be from "old" General Motors (GM). Consider this mission statement of the automaker before its 2009 bankruptcy:

> *"We are a multinational corporation engaged in socially responsible operations, worldwide. We are dedicated to provide products and services of such quality that our customers will receive superior value while our employees and business partners will share in our success and our stockholders will receive a sustained superior return on their investment."*

We consider this a "poor" mission statement because it does not provide a coherent statement of the business definition strategy for the firm. The resulting statement is so vague that it could apply to any large multinational corporation in any industry.

It was statements like old GM's that typified mission statements at the very apex of their silliness. It was as though managers thought that by stringing together some of the most popular biz-buzz of the day, they were truly articulating strategy. The result is a statement so vague that it could apply to any large multinational corporation in any industry.

The good news is that the "new GM," after bankruptcy, no longer posts such nonsense on its website, instead calling itself one of the world's largest automakers, which is exactly how its business definition strategy should be described.

Apple does not provide either a vision or a mission statement.

Google, in contrast, states its mission as follows: "Organize the world's information and make it universally accessible and useful."

Clearly, this is not a description of the Google business definition strategy. It seems more a vision statement because it captures the firm's alpha strategy, technology (the means to organize the world's information), and mentions technology's influencers, namely, business definition ("the world's information") and service delivery ("make it accessible and useful").

I have many concerns about the quality of mission and vision statements I have seen in smaller organizations, whether they be for-profit, not-for-profit, or in the public sector. I think they are a product of the bizarre practice of drafting vision and mission statements as the starting point for thinking about strategy rather than as a final step of summation of conclusions from a process of study and review.

It makes no sense in critical thinking to start with the conclusion of the process without an informed understanding of current strategy and the factors, both internal and external, that are impacting those strategies.

False Alpha

Our second issue with current strategy practices is the use of the false alpha. This occurs when an organization markets a strategy as its alpha even though it is not the organization's alpha.

This practice can make employees and customers cynical because employees and customers know, at least intuitively, what the real alpha strategy is. Don't forget, we believe alpha is reflected in the dominant culture of the organization. Therefore, we think employees and customers can feel the disconnection between what the organization is telling them and what they experience at the organization.

When there is a disconnection between what we are told and what we see happening, the outcome is usually frustration and cynicism. These are not qualities that should be cultivated in employees or customers.

Let's explore the false alpha idea by looking at major banks.

Banks are legendary for the amount of marketing they do to capture customers. The essence of their marketing campaigns is touting the false alpha of customer service (i.e., the service delivery alpha) as though it is the dominant culture of the bank.

Yet a review of any bank website, annual report, and other filings clearly points to financial management as being the alpha. We have made the case already that, because of industry regulatory requirements, the primary focus of banks needs to be on financial management. We could go one step further and also say that risk will always be one of the influencers guiding and constraining financial management implementation.

We have made the case that when financial management is not the alpha for a bank, shareholders, depositors, and regulators should become very concerned. The results have been disastrous. Time has given us plenty of examples of failed banks pursuing an alpha, usually growth, other than financial management. The Icelandic banks come to mind as do Royal Bank of Scotland and Swiss banking giant UBS.

To make it more interesting, service delivery is not even one of the influencers at many banks.

The influencers typically include risk because capital risk is such a huge issue for a bank. The influencers also usually include technology because of regulatory requirements. Data centers at major banks have come to have the look and feel of military installations.

Growth is invariably on the list of influencers even though it almost always plays at backseat role to risk, technology and marketing. Finally, just the size of the marketing effort required to sustain the mirage of customer service as the alpha makes marketing an influencer. The end result is customer service (i.e., service delivery) is invariably an enabler.

Review the annual report of any major bank and you will quickly see the extent of the preoccupation with financial management and risk.

To the extent there is compensation disclosure, you will note that management will be compensated primarily on the performance of capital (financial management). If they are paid bonuses for customer satisfaction measures, the amounts pale in comparison to those awarded for financial management and risk measures.

It would seem that while the banking industry apparently lost its focus on financial management and risk in the years leading up to the financial meltdown in 2008, the industry has now returned to them. The imposition of even more regulations, such as the so-called Volcker Rule in the U.S. aimed at prohibiting certain lines of business, is aligned with our view that financial management should probably be alpha, with risk and technology as the principal influencers.

Financial management, as we have said, focuses on the sourcing, allocation, and management of capital. This is the essence of a bank. The dominant culture is prudent financial management, which often flows from the traditional banker's conservative nature.

That is not to say that a bank cannot deliver excellent service. But we strongly believe that the route to excellent service is not by touting customer service as the bank's alpha.

Because the alpha is financial management, the bank's first priority (and the priority of all its officers and employees) will be preservation of capital; not delivery of customer service.

As an example, consider that it is just not possible to equate a call from a loans officer of the bank, sheepishly demanding repayment of a modest, partially drawn, line of credit from a good borrower for no reason other than this is the edict from head office, is in any way putting the customer first or is a form of service delivery.

Yet this is what banks do time and time again—*to good customers*! And when exactly was the last time a bank said to you, as the customer, "Because we screwed up and put your funds into the wrong account and caused you all the grief that ensued because there were insufficient funds in the account to which we were supposed to deposit the money, we are going to waive all service fees on that account for the next year." The fact is that branch management in banks have almost no leeway in interpreting bank policy. They do as they are told.

What are the implications of this misalignment?

First is that employees tend to treat the mantra that the customer comes first with a degree of skepticism because they know that senior management is rewarded for achieving financial goals and risk measures. They know serving customers is secondary. Serving customers at the branch bank level means absolute adherence to the policy manual and not deviating from that manual to satisfy a customer's need or reality. This is not customer service.

What about customers? Well, the truth is that the differences in customer service among banks are largely imperceptible to them. Customers still pick banks the way they choose cars and credit cards. They are using largely subjective criteria that not even they can fully explain because there are few distinct differences.

So what do we think banks should be doing?

In our opinion, they should be embracing the reality that financial management is their dominant strategy. They should not be denying it or trying to make it look as though customer service is the dominant culture.

They should be identifying the expectations and values that will best guide and constrain the way that dominant strategy and its influencers should impact service delivery.

The point is to turn this apparent weakness (at least in the minds of senior management that want to mask financial management as the dominant strategy) into a strength.

If customers all know that branch managers and loans managers have no authority to deliver true customer service of the sort customers experience in the retail and service industries, then that fact should be accepted by bank management. The service delivery promise of value in a bank can then be about, for example, committing to deliver the required approvals in the shortest time frame possible.

In other words, accept the fact that financial management is the dominant culture and that it imposes very real constraints on the meaning of service delivery within a bank. Design the values and expectations that are consistent with service delivery within that dominant culture.

Employees at a bank already know they are working for a bank. They know the primary objective is preservation of capital. At the branch level, they could still deliver services as professionally as possible in a manner that is consistent with that alpha. Too a large degree, they are already doing it.

But at least they will know they are working in alignment with the bank's stated alpha strategy rather than some marketing campaign of the moment that is not consistent with the culture and dominant strategy of the bank. The employees and customers will be happier. That usually produces better results for everyone.

For another example of false alpha, let's turn back to GE.

Even though the current CEO may make an impassioned pitch, on the GE parent website, about what he is doing to promote growth, we think that growth is not the alpha strategy at GE, the parent.

We believe GE, the parent company, is a banker. At GE, financial management leads with growth and risk as influencers. GE, the parent company, sources capital in capital markets and then, like an investment banker, places huge bets on its business units by allocating capital to them.

The parent, like a banker, sits back and actively manages its investments by setting high growth expectations for each unit. It expects each business unit to be number one in its market and deliver at least an expected minimum return. If the unit can't do that, then the parent will sell it off.

This activity does not make the parent's alpha growth. The parent's alpha is financial management.

The growth expectations imposed on the business units are so aggressive that it makes the whole company seem as though growth is alpha. The reality is that growth is not even the dominant strategy for the business units. Growth is a consequence of the success of their manufacturing and marketing strategies.

I came to this conclusion when I read Jack Welch's book, *Winning* (2005). His three questions for strategy development were: What's the big idea? Who should execute it? How do you do it? Sure sounds to me like the basic business case questions that anyone pitching a venture capitalist has to be able to answer. And that's exactly what it is. I cannot imagine how many pitches Welch must have heard over the years, but that's what he is, a banker, and GE is all about the sourcing, allocation, and management of capital.

The other difficulty I have with the three questions is that each of the GE business units is already up and running. So the three questions are not helpful to them.

Whether it is healthcare, energy, or jet engines, all the business units are way beyond the three questions. Each of those business units needs to understand the expectations imposed on them by GE, their parent company. They need to understand how their current strategies are performing and what factors are or will impact that strategy performance.

This is the information base the business units will use to develop winning strategies. It seems to me that Mr. Welch's three questions are relevant to start-ups and business case preparation because the questions relate to proposing a new product or service and presumably, getting someone to buy-into the idea and fund it. The GE business units are already executing their "ideas".

So what are the consequences to GE from having a false alpha? Well, for one thing, having promoted growth so hard and then being largely unable to achieve it for a host of factors outside the control of management, GE has left shareholders somewhat disappointed in GE performance compared to pre 2008 record. Maybe if the value in the business unit focus was promoted instead, there would be a different expectation.

The other uncomfortable reality from a focus on false alpha is that it is discouraging to employees and management to know intuitively that manufacturing is the dominant alpha while constantly being held to account to the false alpha of growth. We think that can lead to bad decisions. These would be decisions that sacrifice the true dominant strategy priorities in preference for chasing growth.

Let's turn to an example of a company that was a little too successful with promoting growth as its false alpha and is now paying the price. That company is Encana, a publicly traded North American producer of natural gas.

According to its website, Encana is a "high growth, low cost leader in unconventional natural gas production." This statement would seem to indicate growth is the alpha. Certainly, the market bought the story.

Financial management ("low cost") and production ("natural gas production") are presented as influencers. This is a clear, easy to understand statement. As we saw above, such a proposition sets expectations throughout the organization that will be reflected in both business plans and day-to-day operations.

After a great start, Encana's growth strategy stalled because of changes in key external factors, with the primary factor being the collapse of the market price for natural gas.

The growth strategy was predicated on a world with natural gas at historically high prices. With prices falling dramatically from that hoped for reality, the external world has become far less attractive for natural gas producers, making growth problematic until the market starts turning. Encana forecasted high expectations for a U.S. recovery and, by extension, the price of natural gas. Instead, natural gas fell to less than half Encana's prediction. This has reduced the firm's cash flows while forcing it to consider partnerships to reduce the capital spending it needs to push projects to production.

Because we do not believe a production company can have growth as its alpha, Encana's description of its strategy immediately sets off alarm bells for us. In fact, a careful review of the website and securities filings would seem to confirm that production is Encana's actual alpha strategy with financial management and growth as influencers.

The reality is that Encana is paying the price for too strongly promoting growth, which is unfortunate. A review of the financial management strategy reveals very prudent and, some would say, "leading edge" strategies to protect shareholders from the risks of growing too fast and becoming overextended in the process.

If Encana had stated its actual strategy priorities, with production as alpha rather than seeming to have growth as alpha, and with exemplary financial management controls, growth, and technology as influencers, then maybe the Encana story might be different today and the markets might not be so critical of its CEO.

Industry Specific Alphas

We believe that certain industries demand a specific alpha.

We think, within the regulatory industry, risk must be the alpha.

This broad industry characterization is meant to sweep up every "regulator", from those bodies charged with oversight of a self-regulated industry, such as law and bar societies; to classic public sector regulators, such as health and safety inspectors and securities regulators, to the front line regulators; being the police.

I must say, if ever there is a good example of our concept of false alpha, it has to be the decal on police vehicles that so often reads "To Serve and Protect." That's just plain wrong. We want the police to protect first and then to serve.

The first priority for a police force must be to protect. To protect is the first priority for all regulators. It is not to serve.

We think, for example, that risk must be the alpha for every insurance company and pension plan. No other strategy seems appropriate. Insurance and pension plans are all about understanding probabilities and the consequences. That is the foundation on which they base their promise to pay. This means that probability and considerations of consequences ranks ahead of financial management. Financial management becomes an influencer in these companies, but not the alpha.

Let's look at Allstate Insurance Company. In its annual report for 2010, it claims:

> "Allstate is engaged, principally in the United States, in the property liability insurance, life insurance, retirement and investment product business. Allstate's primary business is the sale of private passenger auto and homeowners insurance. The Company also sells several other personal property and casualty insurance products, life insurance, annuities, voluntary accident and health insurance, funding agreements, and select commercial property and casualty coverage."

Risk is present in every statement, which we think is as it should be.

In the same annual report, the CEO writes about "Our Shared Vision"—a strategy to reinvent protection and retirement for the consumer. He says that Allstate placed the customer at the center of the business model (marketing) and created a strategy for risk mitigation to address the difficulties it faced after 2007, a year of difficult growth (growth). Finally, he mentions the financial results (financial management).

Our conclusion from reading this section is that while risk is Allstate's alpha, its influencers are financial management, growth, and marketing. Certainly, we would agree that risk should be alpha and the influencers of financial management, marketing, and growth seem to make sense.

Let's turn to State Farm Insurance Company, the big American life, auto, and casualty insurer. The website for the company describes the mission of

State Farm as risk centered, with phrases such as "helping people manage the risks of everyday life, recover from the unexpected . . . ."

Clearly, risk is the alpha at State Farm. The influencers listed in the State Farm mission, vision, and shared values section, of its website, are marketing, service delivery, and financial management. There is no mention of growth, an influencer mentioned in the Allstate strategy. But then, this is how companies are different from one another. They choose different strategies and priorities and different ways to organize those strategies.

We have already stated our belief that financial management should lead as alpha for all banks, lenders, and hedge funds. After all, financial management is all about the sourcing, allocation, and management of capital. What else could a bank or lender or investment fund have for its alpha strategy?

Growth as alpha strategy has interesting implications for a number of reasons. For instance, we believe it is very challenging, if not impossible, for commodities companies or financial services organizations to have growth as the alpha strategy. For banks or insurance companies, placing growth ahead of financial management (in banks) or risk (in insurance companies) is a challenging, if not a foolhardy, selection for several reasons.

Most compelling, the choice makes growth the first priority, rather than the one on which the organization should focus. Every time we see a bank or an insurer make growth the alpha strategy, we see an unhappy outcome. Recent examples include the experiment that UBS, the venerable Swiss bank, had with growth, which almost ruined it. Then there are those infamous Icelandic banks, whose spectacular collapse in late 2008 signaled the beginning of the global liquidity crisis. Manulife, North America's biggest life insurer, is struggling to cope with a host of issues that arose from more than a decade of focus on growth rather than on risk.

Let's consider the commodities sector; gold producers in particular. To be more specific, let's look only at publicly traded gold producers. Let's pick one that says that growth is its alpha and its vision is to become the biggest producer or to have the largest cash flow per share or the most gold not yet mined.

How will this company implement its strategy? Clearly, one route is through issuance of stock, which, all else equal, will increase market capitalization. With the new capital, the company can acquire additional reserves or production.

Now consider external factors, especially the performance of the capital markets and the price of gold.

In this example, when the most critical and powerful external factors move in a beneficial direction; that is, toward stronger capital markets and higher output commodity prices. Then the growth strategy practically executes itself. Investors happily acquire more and more stock, driving the price up, lowering the company's cost of capital, and so on.

But that is just it. These critical external factors become the driver of growth and management has no control whatsoever over those factors. Conversely, imagine the opposite: falling capital markets and price of gold. The strategy falls apart. The company can no longer issue equity or produce profitable gold.

We believe this is true of most commodity producers, if not all of them. Growth can be a wonderful positive externality but a very dangerous alpha strategy. For growth to dictate the actions of the other seven strategies leaves the firm vulnerable to both positive and negative movements in uncontrollable external factors.

By extension, stakeholders must be very wary of commodity producers that claim growth as their alpha. It is our belief that growth can be the alpha only for organizations that have end user customers. This means growth in a sense that Drucker would understand, namely, as a consequence of customers' valuing the firm's products and services and buying more and more of those products and services. We think this is why McDonald's and Wal-Mart can so successfully pursue growth as their alpha strategy.

In our example, our publicly traded gold producer doesn't have any direct contact with end user customers. Instead, the producer sells its gold to a watchmaker, which then uses the gold to make a watch to sell to an end user customer.

The point is that growth seems sustainable as alpha strategy only when there is an end user customer for the product or service. Customers, like capital markets, are a factor over which management has no control. However, customers and their preferences can be studied and understood. Customer relationships can be developed. In short, customers provide a much more workable foundation for growth.

CHAPTER 6
ALPHA RISK MANAGEMENT

Risk Management is a Strategy Review

The Alpha Strategies model brings a new perspective to risk management practices by treating risk management as a review of strategy.

Consider this analogy to understand the difference between the way we see current practices and what we are proposing. Present risk management practices seem to us to be comparable to studying a photograph of a river for risks. The river becomes a metaphor for a world of risks we cannot control. We can imagine all sorts of risks associated with the river.

The use of The Alpha Model approach adds strategy to the picture of the river. The essence of The Alpha Strategies model is enabling connections to be made between strategy and factors impacting strategy performance. For example, what risks does our marketing strategy face? What risks does our service delivery strategy face?

The Alpha Strategies model can be used to connect specific strategies to specific risks threatening the success of those strategies. As such, risk management becomes a strategy review because it asks the question "Is our strategy still appropriate if the risks it now faces have changed dramatically from the assumptions about risk that supported strategy implementation?"

For purposes of our photograph analogy, consider now that we are looking at exactly the same photo of the river, as before, only now the photo includes some folks in a boat on that river.

Before, we were looking at just a photo of a river, representing risk. In other words, we were looking at risk in isolation. Now we are looking at a picture of some people in a boat on the river. The people in the boat represent strategy. Now we have a picture that shows risk, being the river, framed in the context of a strategy, being people in a boat on the river.

The picture of just the river tells us very little about the risks the river poses. Including the image of the people boating on the river tells us much more.

If we were to conduct a risk analysis by studying our fictional photo more closely, we might notice, say, that some of the boaters aren't wearing life jackets. We might also note that there seem to be too many people in the boat. It is the relationship between risk (the river) and strategy (boating on the river) that enables us to identify the obvious risks the river presents because we can see the two, risk and strategy, together. As a result, now we can identify the possible risk of capsizing because the boat seems overloaded. We can also identify the possible risk of drowning because the people in the boat do not appear to be wearing life jackets.

This is what The Alpha Strategies approach brings to a risk management discussion. It frames the discussion of risk against specific strategies thereby converting the discussion into a review of strategy. We are no longer looking for risks in isolation. We are looking for risks to chosen strategy.

Strategy must be included in any discussion of risk because strategy is always set by reference to risk. We define risk as being any factor outside the control of a manager. Strategy, on the other hand, is something under the control of a manager and we have defined it as a chosen course of action. Inherent in a manager's choice of action (strategy) are assumptions about uncontrollable factors.

In other words, inherent in the choice of action, being strategy, are assumptions about risk. In our boating picture analogy, the assumptions relevant to the boating strategy seem to be that the boat can handle the number of people in it and will not easily capsize and that life jackets are not necessary. We can now test those assumptions and determine if they are still appropriate. If they are not still appropriate, we can discuss how we need to modify our strategy to address our new understanding of the risks our strategy faces.

Let's move away from our river photograph analogy and frame the risk discussion against an actual strategy. Let's say that a manager decides to develop a financing strategy to take advantage of the availability of capital and favorable interest rates.

The choice of financing strategy is under the control of the manager. Favorable interest rates and availability of capital are the factors not under the control of the manager. The strategy is set by reference to those uncontrollable factors. The success of the financing strategy will become absolutely dependent on the assumptions made about the availability of capital and favorable interest rates because these assumptions are about the risks the financing strategy faces.

These assumptions will likely include deciding how long capital will remain available and interest rates will stay attractive. The manager will use these assumptions to inform strategy implementation decisions, such as "Should we refinance all our assets at once in one loan or will capital and interest rate conditions remain the same long enough to allow us to refinance each asset individually?" As the manager sees those assumptions changing for better or worse, the manager will adjust strategies accordingly.

The difficulty we have with popular current risk practices is that they attempt to identify risk without understanding strategies and assumptions about risk that have already been made in choosing those strategies. In other words, these practices focus on just risk without relating it to relevant strategy.

For example, typical current risk management methodology suggests that the process should begin with an understanding of some vague, ominous sounding definition for risk. The next step usually involves brainstorming with managers to generate large lists of potential risks. These lists never have any context in that they are never related to actual specific strategies.

This is then followed by the advice to prioritize those risks using severity of impact and probability of occurrence to do so. How this can be done without reference to specific strategies is beyond our understanding. The final step in current practices is to develop action plans to manage the selected risks. This makes the action plans seem so detached from reality, in our opinion, that they are akin to rearranging the deck chairs on the Titanic rather than keeping watch for icebergs.

We do not believe in the current practice of scanning the universe for risks. The universe is too large with too many risks in it, making the practice comparable to looking for a needle in a haystack.

Our approach is to understand current strategies first. That understanding enables identification of the fundamental assumptions about risk made when those strategies were first chosen. Those assumptions on risk can then be reviewed against a changing external reality and new risks, if any, that are appearing on the scene.

Strategy Choices Create Risks

We are going to look at how the choice of strategy in a major capital infrastructure project (e.g., a bridge or a hospital or a mine shaft) impacts the identification and management of risk.

A typical major project offers a wonderfully simple perspective on strategy and risks to that strategy because conventional thinking on project management would have us believe that project management involves balancing the three typical expectations of budget, schedule, and scope.

Budget represents a strategy to complete the project on or under budget. Schedule represents a strategy to finish the project on or ahead of schedule. Finally, scope represents a strategy to complete the project to meet expected design and operating requirements.

The typical image offered to display the relationship of these common expectations is a perfect equilateral triangle with budget, schedule, and scope as the points of the triangle, as shown in Figure 22.

Figure 22 Typical Presentation of Competing Project Priorities

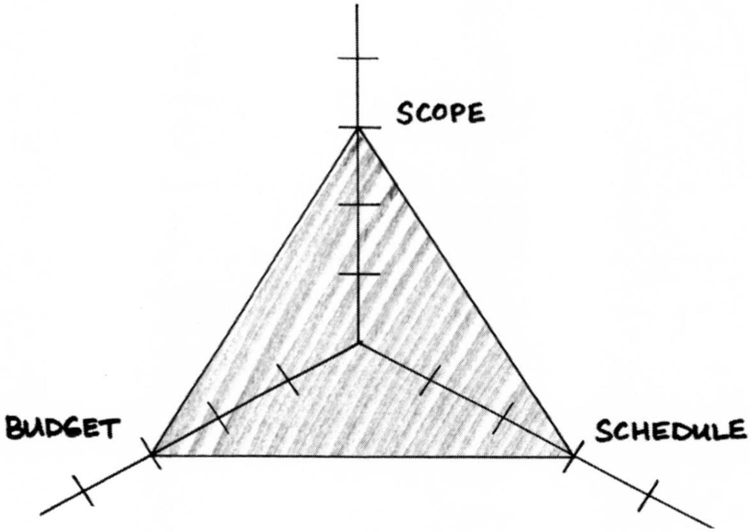

Experienced project managers know that the unique nature of each project is created by the priority of expectations imposed on them, as project managers. They know that they must push the project's sponsor to identify which expectation is paramount in importance. They know that one and only one of these expectations can be the strategy for the project.

The choice of that strategy will determine the way the project will be managed because risks will vary depending on the strategy chosen.

Let's prove this assertion by looking at each of the typical strategies of cost, schedule, and scope as the possible chosen strategy for our project example. This exercise will demonstrate the impact the choice of strategy makes to risk identification and management.

Let's assume that budget (cost) is the project priority and the chosen strategy. In other words, cost is to be paramount throughout the project delivery.

This means that the strategy driving all project management decisions will be to achieve the prescribed cost. Anything that could threaten the budget and cost strategy is a risk that must be identified and addressed. These risks include missing any opportunity to reduce cost. Cost becomes more important than meeting the schedule and more important than delivery of the project's scope.

To calibrate the impact of the choice of budget as the strategy, in Figure 23, we have added hash marks to the lines originating from the center of the triangle and penetrating each of the three points of it, being marked as budget, schedule, and scope. We then assigned the numerical value 3 to each point where the line intersects each of the points of the triangle.

Figure 23 Budget as the Project Priority

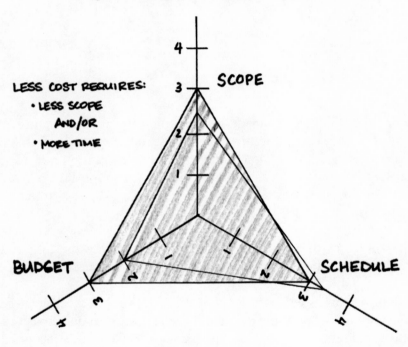

In a perfect world with everything going according to plan, budget would achieve a value of 3 or perhaps less than 3, meaning that the project was completed at budgeted cost or less. Schedule and scope would each achieve a 3. However, the world is far from ideal. As the project manager struggles to mitigate risks to the budget in order to achieve a cost at completion of 3 on our scale, we watch as the schedule may extend beyond its point of the triangle to 3.25 and scope may slip down to about 2.5.

This is shown in Figure 23 by the scalene triangle that appears inside the equilateral triangle resulting from plotting the actual achieved results for each of the three. Why did the final results produce a scalene triangle rather than the planned equilateral one? In particular, what has happened to schedule and scope? Why did schedule become a 3.25? Why did scope drop to 2.5? Why has neither of schedule nor scope achieved the planned value of 3?

The answer to these questions is that the risks to budget were managed at the expense of risks to the other strategies. Risks to schedule and scope were secondary to risks to achieving budget. Budget was the priority and expectation and therefore budget became the project alpha. For purposes of risk identification, risk can now be tied to the strategy of achieving budget. If budget is paramount, then the risk focus must be to identify and address all possible risks to budget.

In our example, the schedule is extended to a 3.25 because meeting schedule required too much cost. Scope dropped to 2.5 because scope had to be reduced in order to stay on budget.

For example, a significant risk to budget in major capital projects comes from not understanding the risks each of the many cost elements face. For example, the cost of steel could double. The site might require unforeseen and expensive environmental remediation. Any project truly having cost as the number one priority should be subjected to significant costing studies in order to identify and understand the risks cost faces and how to address those cost risks.

Once the paramount strategy is chosen, it becomes possible to understand how to identify and prioritize risks to that strategy. There are risks everywhere. Without strategy as a reference point, it is very easy to identify very real but completely irrelevant risks to the project's success, which, in this case, means achieving budget.

Now, let's change our example project strategy to that of schedule. If want to achieve a schedule strategy or even come in ahead of schedule, the project manager must identify the risks to schedule. The consequences of managing these risks to schedule are that budget and scope are likely to suffer.

The scalene triangle inside the equilateral triangle of Figure 24 shows the impact of schedule as the strategy. We can see that schedule has achieved the 2 value as we raced to achieve no more than a 3 and brought the project in ahead of schedule. Scope has dropped to 2.25 because there wasn't time to complete all the required scope in order to meet the required completion date.

But the project is a success because it came ahead of schedule. Budget finishes at a 4.1 because additional costs required to complete on schedule caused a budget overrun.

Figure 24 Schedule as the Project Priority

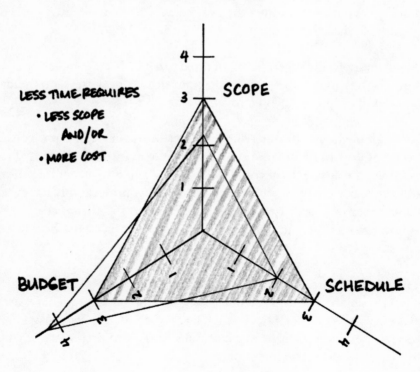

If you think about it, schedule is the principal strategy driving almost all military projects.

If the army needs a bridge across the river during a campaign, the last thing the military worries about is "Why did this bridge cost so much and why isn't it finished to specifications?"

The military would only worry about how quickly the bridge can be ready.

The third choice of possible strategy in our triangle example is scope. Scope can drive the project and be the paramount strategy.

Examples of scope driven projects could be a pharmaceutical research project or maybe putting man on the moon. For purposes of our example, we will use the building of the CN Tower which opened in Toronto in 1976.

The CN Tower is an excellent example of a scope driven project. After all, it was intended to be the tallest structure in the world, and for decades held that record. The structure was known from the start to be a one of a kind. It was built to be a broadcasting antenna higher than the tallest buildings in the City of Toronto at that time.

As such, it would overcome the interference caused by downtown skyscrapers to the transmission of broadcast signals throughout the city. But the tower quickly became seen as something more. As the world's tallest structure, it had the potential to become a major global tourist attraction.

Consider the implications of choosing scope as strategy.

You would never hear someone say: "What do you mean you want to cap off the CN Tower at 800 feet instead of taking it to 1,800 feet because you'll be over budget. It cannot function as a broadcasting antenna at 800 feet!"

As a result, a scope project is more likely to produce a scalene triangle of actual values as is shown in the Figure 25 below.

Figure 25 Scope as the Project Priority

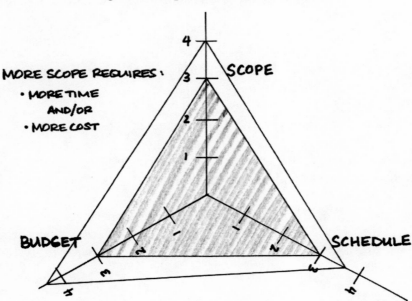

We can see both schedule and budget pushing out beyond the planned value of 3 for each. Schedule came in at 3.5 and budget was pushed to 4.25. In fact, the scope value also increased beyond 3 to a value of 4 as the scope continually increased with a better understanding of what the potential of the project could be and the challenges in designing and building a one of a kind structure.

As an example of unforeseen scope challenges, the final spire for the structure had to be lowered onto the top of the structure from a Sikorsky helicopter because there was no other way to install it.

The lessons demonstrated from managing risk in projects are applicable to all strategy plans, from the strategic plan to business plans, to any plan to implement strategy. The identification and management of risk must include relevant strategy. Risk management is, in fact, a review of strategy.

Alpha Risks

Let's look at risk from the perspective of each of the eight alpha strategies as another means to demonstrate the link between risk and strategy. Not surprisingly, the risks faced by each of The Alpha Strategies are quite different.

Risk

The risk strategy focuses on the identification and management of threats to the success of the organization. We think a threat can include a missed opportunity. Risk is the alpha or dominant strategy for insurers, pension funds, and regulators.

For an insurer, the risk is that it does not understand the probability or the consequences of the risks that it has underwritten. As a result, for example, the list of exclusions to even a simple homeowner's fire insurance seems to increase each year as the property insurer increases its understanding of potential risks of fire in the home.

For a pension fund, a big risk realized in recent years has been the impact of the increasing life expectancy of its pension plan beneficiaries. The emergence of that factor has required pension plans to scramble to modify the plans they are administering.

For regulators, the major risk is missing emerging sources of risk to the stakeholders the regulator is mandated to protect. The S.E.C. was criticized for not identifying that Bernie Madoff was a fraudster until Madoff's Ponzi scheme, the biggest in American history, collapsed at the cost of the life savings of thousands of investors.

Financial Management

Financial management addresses the sourcing, allocation, and management of capital. This should be the alpha for all banks, lenders, and probably most investment managers and hedge funds.

The risks are inherent in the description of the strategy. What if capital cannot be sourced? That's a big risk. Isn't this at the heart of the 2012 Eurozone crisis, with country after country scrambling to raise capital to refinance its sovereign debt?

There are the risks associated with allocating capital. The corporate landscape is littered with corporate CEO's whose biggest bets, usually acquisitions, saw the value of their target, as well as their own careers and reputations, disappear in the months after the acquisition.

Consider the $37 billion Mercedes Benz merger with Chrysler in 1998. By 2007, Daimler Benz had sold Chrysler for $7 billion. Sears merged with Kmart in 2005. Today in 2012, Kmart no longer exists and Sears has announced over one hundred stores will be closed. Then there is the Snapple story. Quaker Oats, the porridge people, bought Snapple, a fruit drink company, for $1.7 billion in 1994 and sold it about two years later for something like $300 million!

The final element of financial management is management of capital. A major risk in management of capital is fraud. UBS, the big Swiss bank, lost over $2 billion because of a rogue trader in its London office.

Service Delivery / Production / Manufacturing
Service delivery, which can also be production or manufacturing, is all about fulfilling the marketing promise, including the warranty obligations.

Whenever we think of risks to fulfilling the marketing promise, the words negligent or defective come to mind. Consider the risks in manufacturing and the automakers. Toyota recalled nearly 1.7 million vehicles in 2011 alone. Ford had to recall more than 14 million trucks and SUVs in 2008 and 2009 to replace faulty cruise controls.

Both manufacturing and production are responsible for some horrific environmental messes, a consequence of practices for the most part no longer considered acceptable or even legal.

So much for manufacturers and production companies, let's look at some of the biggest service delivery organizations, namely, governments.

The financial woes of the city of Harrisburg, the capital of Pennsylvania, are a direct result of not understanding the risks inherent in a project to refurbish and repurpose the city's incinerator with a new cogeneration capability that was to be a big new revenue source for the city. The project was to cost some $70 million in 2003. As of November 2011, the city has had to go into bankruptcy, with something like $310 million of debt attributable to the project, which still isn't functioning.

Marketing

Marketing is all about identifying and capturing customers and clients with a promise of value in the organization's goods and services.

Companies with marketing as their alpha include retailers, soft drink makers and most beer companies, and consumer goods firms, such as Proctor and Gamble or consumer pharmaceuticals such as Johnson & Johnson. Public sector examples include government run lottery companies. Many not-for-profit organizations which serve as the "voice" for their members by promoting awareness of what their members do have marketing as their alpha.

The risks facing this alpha are that the market doesn't like what is being marketed to them. Consider "New Coke", the ill-fated attempt by Coca-Cola to rebrand its famous soft drink.

Then there is the risk of not understanding the market demand. The British division of Hoover Vacuum Cleaner Company started a marketing promotion in 1992 that ended badly with the forced sale of the firm. Apparently, when Hoover offered free airplane tickets to customers buying more than £100 of its products, it had not anticipated that some people would purchase appliances just for the free plane tickets. The obligation to provide free tickets overwhelmed Hoover, which had to be restructured and sold to escape these liabilities.

The story is very relevant to merchants wishing to attract customers using Groupon, the Internet based marketing phenomenon. Groupon negotiates bulk discounts from merchants and then offers those deals through e-mail based marketing. Unfortunately, like Hoover Vacuum Cleaner, some merchants have badly underestimated the power of the Groupon marketing scheme and have been overwhelmed with the ensuing discount business.

Growth

Growth is all about the focus on the type and rate of growth. The type of growth typically is categorized as internal growth or external growth, being acquisitions, partnerships, franchising, strategic alliances, and the like.

Examples of companies with growth as their alpha include Walt-Mart. The biggest single risk these companies face is the loss of the ability to manage the ever expanding company. This may lead to ever more questionable decision making and eventually even to collapse. At the time of this writing, Wal-Mart has suffered a drop in its share price that has taken ten billion dollars off the value of its market capitalization. Apparently, there were questionable payments being made in foreign jurisdictions and an investigation is underway on the matter.

Drucker worried in 1954 about these issues when he wrote *The Practice of Management*. He was thinking about internal growth, not growth by acquisitions, which is a much faster route to expansion. We would point out that the corporate landscape is littered with the ruins of companies that grew too fast, lost control, and were ruined because factors in the external environment, such as capital availability, were risks that these companies either ignored or hoped would never occur.

R&D / technology

R&D / technology strategy is concerned with the creation and use of intellectual capital, being either proprietary products or services or both for the purpose of enabling productivity and producing competitive advantage for the organization. Those organizations with R&D / technology as their alpha include many pharmaceutical and technology firms. Public sector and not-for-profit examples include universities and government research bodies such as NASA.

The obvious risk facing this alpha is that the intellectual capital created is considered of little or no value or out of date by the market for which it is intended. At the time of this writing, the venerable photographic equipment company, Kodak, has filed for bankruptcy, having fallen victim to that risk. Research in Motion, inventor of the BlackBerry, is scrambling because some of its latest product launches have not enjoyed the success of those of its competitors.

Another risk, and the worst nightmare for pharmaceutical firms, is that the developed product produces unforeseen and disastrous side effects. Or the technology doesn't function as planned, as was the case for the disastrous launch of a Space Shuttle Challenger flight in 1986 that resulted in the deaths of all seven astronauts on board the vehicle.

Organization Management

The strategy is about the sourcing, allocation, and management of human capital, being the personnel requirements required by the firm. When this strategy is used as alpha, this strategy becomes the "selfish" strategy. Its focus is on people; usually meaning the founder or personality of the firm. We see this strategy as alpha in law firms and architectural firms where the firm is known by the persona of its principal partner rather than for the firm itself.

Of course, the risk facing this strategy, as alpha, is that if anything happens to the driving force and face of the business, the business is essentially out of business. Donald Trump, wheeler-dealer and sometime reality T.V. show host, comes to mind, as does Frank Gehry, the famous architect of buildings lacking in anything like a straight edge, David Hockney, the artist, and Tom Cruise, actor and producer extraordinaire.

Business Definition / Mandate

The business definition strategy is concerned with the positioning of the firm in the competitive environment.

The big risk is in not understanding how the firm is actually positioned. This leads to identification of the wrong competitors and wrong factors shaping ongoing change in the industry.

The organizations with Business Definition as their alpha are focused on constantly adjusting their positioning in the competitive environment. The risk these organizations face is that they may not fully understand what each apparent opportunity requires in order to achieve success with it.

CHAPTER 7
ALPHA CULTURE AND VALUES

The Alpha Cultures

Have you ever wondered why, when you walk into the offices of some organizations, you sometimes feel instantly uncomfortable? Or maybe just the opposite happens and you love the atmosphere? That's the dominant culture you are sensing and either you like it a lot or you don't like it at all.

If you are a marketing and sales type and venture into a room full of bankers, you will notice the difference in cultures. What you are experiencing is a marketing culture running up against a finance culture. Or how about entering a police station, just to ask a simple question? If risk isn't your thing, you probably won't feel comfortable there because risk is the dominant culture for all police forces.

The chart below takes a tongue in cheek look at descriptions of the general culture across each of the eight strategies *when that strategy is the lead or alpha strategy for the organization as a whole.*

Figure 26 The Alpha Cultures

THE ALPHA STRATEGIES	ALPHA CULTURE IN A SOUND BYTE
BUSINESS DEFINITION	"WE SHOULD BE MOVING INTO THAT BUSINESS"
RISK	"WHAT ARE THE CHANCES OF THAT HAPPENING"?
GROWTH	"WE ARE GOING TO NEED A LOT MORE SPACE – SOON!"
FINANCIAL MANAGEMENT	"CAN YOU CHECK THOSE NUMBERS AGAIN?"
R+D / TECHNOLOGY	"HAVE WE EVER LOOKED AT DOING IT THIS WAY?"
ORGANIZATION MANAGEMENT	"WHAT'S IN IT FOR ME?"
MARKETING	"REBRAND IT AND IT WILL SELL ITSELF"
SERVICE DELIVERY / PRODUCTION / MANUFACTURING	"WE CAN DO THAT RIGHT AWAY. NO PROBLEM!"

We are going to look at each of the eight strategies as being the alpha strategy for an organization to see if we can identify some behaviors closely associated with those strategies.

Service Delivery / Production / Manufacturing

Service delivery as alpha has the culture of "We can do that right away. No problem!"

In the private sector, service delivery includes production and manufacturing. There are service firms such as the parcel delivery companies FedEx, Purolator, and UPS (United Parcel Services). Four Seasons Hotels competes with other hotel chains on the superior level of its services.

To show how service delivery can shape the culture of an organization, let me tell a story. I can remember riding in an elevator with the president of a large property management firm. You could certainly tell he embodied the company's alpha strategy of service delivery. When the elevator doors opened to the lobby, he saw a piece of scrap of paper on the floor. He stepped off the elevator and stopped the people behind him from leaving the elevator until he had a chance to bend over and pick up the scrap and put it into the trash receptacle.

I can remember thinking to myself that his actions explained why many observers considered the company the nation's best property manager. Its president set the tone and culture for excellence in service delivery, its alpha strategy.

Financial Management

Financial management has a culture of "Can you check those numbers again?"

Financial management is the alpha for banks and investment firms. Most governments around the world impose varying tests for sufficiency and adequacy of capital on banks, making financial management, as alpha, absolutely essential. Fail those tests, and the regulator can put a bank out of business. No wonder bankers are obsessed with numbers.

The banking business is founded on leveraging capital. As a result, the margins for error and profit are small (with the happy exception, at least to a banker, of fees charged for services). Many people will think "Mr. Monopoly", the rotund, mustachioed banker gentleman of the game bearing his name serves as a good image for the culture of financial management.

Marketing

Marketing has the culture of "Rebrand it and it will sell itself!"

Well known companies with marketing as alpha include Apple and firms in the beverage industry, such as Coca-Cola and Pepsi. These are global enterprises enjoying extensive brand recognition.

Lots of not-for-profits have marketing as alpha strategy. Whether it is Easter Seals or the United Way, these charities use marketing to excite and inspire volunteers to do the work and collect the money. Lottery corporations have marketing as their alpha strategy, whether they are government run or in the private sector. The promise is the chance of realizing the dream of becoming a millionaire instantly!

Let's take a look at how Scott Adams's comic strip *Dilbert* captures a tongue in cheek picture of the culture in a marketing organization.

In one of my favorite Dilbert strips, a marketing/sales guy asks Dilbert, the engineer/techie, to go on a sales call with him. Dilbert rolls his eyes at the request. In the car, en route to the sales call, the sales guy asks Dilbert to describe the product they will be pitching to the prospective customer. Dilbert rolls his eyes again, no doubt asking himself why the sales guy hasn't bothered to find out this information until now. But Dilbert decides to give an answer and says, "It runs on software and uses electricity." The marketing/sales guy immediately throws up his hands and exclaims, "Information overload!" There is a look of pure disdain on Dilbert's face because he has so much difficulty relating to the marketing culture, a culture that is much less concerned with details than Dilbert, than the technology engineer is.

Marketing cultures are not known for attention to detail. They are known for making the pitch.

Growth
Growth has the culture of "We're going to need a lot more space—soon!"

There are two kinds of growth companies. There are those that grow as a consequence of the success of their products and services. Then there are those that grow by acquisitions.

The challenge with any significant growth is addressing concerns about the ability of management and the board to manage the ever growing organization. The culture at a growth firm reflects this constant awareness of the need to anticipate the requirements of growth.

McDonald's and Wal-Mart are quintessential internal growth companies. They address these concerns with a continuing commitment to employee training and development. McDonald's has its Hamburger University, which is in its fiftieth year of operation, and Wal-Mart runs an extensive program of training and career development.

The common characteristic of an organization leading with growth is an unrelenting commitment to growth. For a growth company, the downturn in one market simply drives the focus onto other markets.

The unfortunate reality is that having growth as the alpha strategy is similar to having skydiving as a hobby. Growth, like skydiving, can be an exhilarating sport. But it can be deadly because it is all or nothing. The acquisition takes very little time. Productive integration of the acquisition into the buyer's organization is the killer. There is a long list of spectacular collapses of companies that could not accept the reality that growth was no longer a sustainable alpha.

R&D / Technology

The R&D / technology culture can be summed up with "Have we ever looked at doing it this way?"

This is the culture of intellectual curiosity best epitomized by "geeks" and "nerds", also known as "rocket scientists". Sergey Brin, one of the founders of Google, would no doubt consider himself a nerd, as would Mark Zuckerberg, the founder of Facebook.

There are many examples of public sector organizations with R&D / technology as alpha. Two of my favorites are the (U.S.) National Aeronautics and Space Administration (NASA) and Canada's National Research Council (NRC).

If ever I feel the need to be inspired, I just visit the NASA website! NASA's vision statement is pure research: "To reach for new heights and reveal the unknown so that what we do and learn will benefit all humankind." Now that's an alpha strategy.

Risk

The risk strategy culture can be described in this sentence: "What are the chances of that happening?" Risk is all about the ongoing consideration of probabilities and consequences.

Risk is the alpha for pension funds and for insurers. We would also argue that risk is the alpha strategy for many investment banks and hedge funds.

Goldman Sachs, as an investment bank now converted to a bank, is famous, perhaps now infamous, for its obsession with risk.

When *The Economist* runs an issue with a front cover screaming "Goldman Sachs: A Culture of Risk," you have to believe that risk is the firm's alpha strategy. To reinforce the headline, the cover picture showed a mountain climber dangling on the end of a rappelling rope against the backdrop of a spectacular vista of mountaintops.

William D. Cohan in *Money and Power: How Goldman Sachs Came to Rule the World (2011)*, asks whether the company succeeded because it was better than everyone else or just very good at cheating. I wonder whether Cohan got it right the first time. I wonder whether Goldman was and is better than everyone else because Goldman understands that risk is a strategy to manage, has made risk its alpha and culture, and just seems to be able to manage the risk strategy better than anyone else.

Risk is the alpha strategy for those public sector organizations that regulate. Think of the police. The slogan on most police cars is usually "To Serve and Protect." We think the police culture is better reflected by changing the word order to: "To Protect and then to Serve." Protection will always come before service delivery.

Business Definition
The business definition culture is summed up with: "We should be moving into that business."

As alpha for an organization, business definition is the strategy of reinvention, enabling the organization to "morph" into the next version of itself. The focus is on an ongoing repositioning of the firm, almost to the point where, notwithstanding that customers and clients may love the firm; they are unable to really describe what it does.

For example, Canada's Thomson Corporation, until the 1990s, was one of the world's largest owners of hard copy professional information, having a variety of textbook and reference materials, for lawyers, accountants and other professionals. Then in the 1990s, once the potential of the Internet became clear, Thomson decided to morph into digital information. After more than ten years of implementation, Thomson Corporation has transformed itself into one of the world's largest owners of digital information. Just as folks began to understand that Thomson had swapped hard copy for soft copy (i.e., paper for digital), it went and bought Reuters, a global newswire service and provider of data about financial markets, changing once again our understanding of the now Thomson Reuters.

We know of no public sector use of mandate as alpha. We have met plenty of bureaucrats who would take issue with that statement. Their line of reasoning turns on their belief that they cannot undertake anything except what is addressed in the mandate. Therefore, they argue that their mandate must be alpha. This is a flawed argument because their mandate is invariably embedded in a statute, and typically directs their organizations to be, for example, a regulator (risk as alpha) or to deliver services (service delivery as alpha). Mandate will be an influencer at best.

Organization Management
The organization management culture is best described as "What's in it for me?"

Organization is not a common alpha. That's because it is truly a selfish strategy. It's for organizations whose personnel look after their interests first. That's right. These people are almost "lone wolves" or "guns for hire" who have banded together in a loose confederation for as long as that association is giving them what they want. Or they run their own business, basing it on their reputation. They have no need to look after anyone else, and if the organization does not address their needs then they pack their bags and move to one that will.

So who would these folks be? Many law firms still provide a prime example of organization management as alpha. Many law firm partners are not yet part of a faceless brand, as tends to happen at the major management consulting, accounting, and engineering services firms. Law partners can still gather up their clients and take them elsewhere when they become unhappy with their treatment at their present firm. The client wants the partner, not the firm. That's the hallmark of an organization management driven firm.

The same can be seen in many architecture and design and advertising firms. For example, clients want Frank Gehry, designer of the Balboa museum, known for its aerodynamic design. They don't want a design firm. They want Frank Gehry.

Organization could be the alpha for some entertainment companies. For example, when season tickets are going up for sale, the Stratford Shakespeare Festival in Stratford, Ontario, takes out a two page color advertisement in major newspapers showing the actors it has signed to play in the coming season. People went to see *Hamlet* at Winnipeg's Manitoba Theatre Centre years ago not because of the play but to see Keanu Reeves in the title role. And they did so in droves.

The Present Approach to Values is Inadequate

Let us start with our definition of values.

Values, within the context of strategic management, are expectations imposed on managers and employees by the strategic plan. These expectations are focused on describing the characteristics that individuals are expected to exhibit in their behaviors and decision making as they carry out their responsibilities with respect to strategy implementation. We think the term, values, is synonymous with culture.

We believe that the present approach to articulating values and principles is inadequate for two reasons.

First, it typically addresses only values associated with the organization management strategy (i.e., people) and does not address the values for the remaining seven strategies.

Secondly, the present approach identifies "hoped for" values without first understanding the current values reflecting strategy implementation. The term "values and principles" should reflect behaviors that employees and managements are expected to exhibit when implementing the organization's strategy. What we see, more often than not, is that stated values of the organization are not the practiced values.

We believe that identification of values, much the same as identification of risk, must start with understanding the strategies currently in place in an organization and, in particular, the alpha strategy. Once those current strategies are understood, then it is possible to identify the values that are characterizing implementation of them.

The alpha or lead strategy drives a dominant culture which, in turn, allows us to identify Apple, the technology firm, for example, as being driven by marketing, banks by financial management, insurers and regulators by risk, most manufacturers as production, and so on.

The unique way each organization implements alpha gives the organization its unique identity. Values are very much a part of that strategy implementation process. Moreover, the values necessary to guide implementation of an alpha strategy of, say, risk are quite different from those that influence the implementation of, say, marketing.

The conventional wisdom on planning seems to tell us we have to set values before strategy. This suggests a complete misunderstanding of strategy and its origins.

When entrepreneurs start companies, they embed their personal values into every strategy they implement. It is impossible to determine which came first: the idea for the strategy or the value system of the entrepreneur. Entrepreneurs have clear expectations for how they expect each of their chosen strategies to be executed. Over time, these expectations become entrenched. The values may evolve or change over time. But values, just like strategy, are already in place in every organization that is a going concern.

We believe the question that all organizations must ask themselves is "What are the organization's values right now?"

This does not mean asking what employees want the values to be or what management thinks they should be.

The question seeks a description of the current values. We believe that there is no sense exploring the possibility of new values without understanding the current ones. What are the values already in place the organization?

Once those values are understood, then we can ask the questions whether they are consistent with current alpha strategy and its influencers and enablers.

I love the story about the new greeter at a local Wal-Mart store because it speaks so well to a store manager who understands which values are important to the store's success.

The manager called in a new employee, an elderly, distinguished looking gentleman, at the end of his first week. The manager had concerns about the new employee's inability to show up at work on time.

The new fellow was usually no more than fifteen minutes late, but this was his first week, and the tardiness worried the manager. Customers appeared to like the new greeter very much. So did the staffers with whom he worked. They had no complaints whatsoever. The manager decided to start what he thought might be a difficult discussion with a direct question. He asked the new hire, "What did they do in your last job if you showed up late?"

The man smiled and replied, "Usually, they said, 'Good morning, Admiral. Would you like your coffee now?'"

In a heartbeat, the store manager knew he had to decide which values were more important to his management of the store. There was his desire to have all his employees show up for work at the same prescribed time or he could have happy customers and good relations amongst the staff by accommodating the Admiral's tardiness. It seemed to him unlikely that he could have both, particularly with this employee.

It was an easy decision, guided by the expectation imposed on the store manager to create a friendly and welcoming retail environment for shoppers. The store manager chose to ignore the Admiral's tardiness. I have a picture in my mind of the store manager then becoming truly engrossed in listening to one of the Admiral's many stories.

The point of the story is that each organization expects employees to behave in a certain way when they are implementing the organization's strategies. This is the idea we are exploring here. We are not proposing doing away with values. That would be impossible to do. In the absence of explicit direction on how to implement a given strategy, the employee will usually do it their way in accordance with what they believe and value.

We don't think organizations are harnessing even a fraction of the power of values because, as with our risk management practices, we are separating values from the strategy to which they best relate.

Look at the findings of the Boston Research Group which surveyed thousands of American employees at every level on the subject of performance management. Broadly speaking, the research found that 97 percent of organizations still manage from the top down, using command and control or what the researchers termed informed acquiescence.

Only 3 percent of organizations have self-governance in which employees actually believe the company operates consistently with its values and follow those practices.

Other findings include that 90 percent of the self-governance group (being 3 percent of the total groups surveyed) would blow the whistle on their firm if necessary. In the other groups, less than 25 percent would do so. So much for managing ethics and compliance!

Ninety percent of the self-governance group agree that their company readily adopts good ideas. In the other two groups, 20 percent believe this. What a comment on the opportunity to improve implementation of strategy!

But here are the real eye-openers.

Only twenty-seven percent of bosses believe their firm inspires its employees. (I guess that means the other 73 percent do not believe the message themselves.) Meanwhile, only 4 percent of employees agree that their firm inspires them. Forty-one percent of bosses say their company rewards performance on values rather than on financial measures. Only 14 percent of employees agree.

These findings say to us that today's approach to values just isn't working!

This would seem to explain why so many value statements hanging in the lobbies of various organizations are generally regarded as meaningless. According to the Boston Research Group findings, employees don't believe in them. What this tells me is that the values described on the websites and annual reports of most organizations do not represent the values present in the organization. But I get the feeling that I am not telling the reader anything they don't know already. So let's get started on a solution.

Identify Strategy First, Then Values

We believe it is not possible to set values first and then strategy.

The only time this happens, in our opinion, is when a new organization is founded. If it is a for-profit entity, you will definitely see the entrepreneur's values stamped on the start-up. If sponsors create a new not-for-profit organization, the sponsor's values will be part and parcel of the new organization's strategies. If elected officials mandate through law the creation of a new public sector vehicle to administer a statute, then you will be hard-pressed to separate the values and strategies and which came first.

But once an organization has been up and running and those founding fathers have disappeared, what we see is that the values change. Or, at the very least, folks working at those organizations can no longer agree on what the values are.

At this point in an organization's life cycle, it is inappropriate and problematic to consider setting values first and then setting strategy. Values are a form of expectations and serve as direction on how strategy is to be implemented. Therefore, values must be set after strategy is set.

Consider an organization with a mandate to be both a new home warranty vendor and the industry regulator in the new home building industry. Both of these roles require risk to be the alpha strategy. But implementation of that strategy is also very different for each.

When the organization was created thirty years ago, the decision was made to have the regulatory role be the primary tool to manage industry standards and risk. The warranty role was very much a secondary tool. After some twenty-five years of success, the organization was able to move to a reversal of those priorities by moving the regulatory role to the secondary position.

The implications for culture change at the organization were enormous. Basically, the organization was changing from a police mentality to an insurer's mentality.

The implications for setting values are enormous. If the organization was to set its values before deciding on a change in its risk strategy, then it likely would have set the values of a regulator.

Think about the difference in the values of a regulator as compared to those of an insurer.

A regulator has the values of a police service. In a regulator's mind, there are good guys and bad guys. The values of an insurer focus the likelihood and consequence of the occurrence of risk and the needs of the insured parties when those risks occur.

An insurer, on the other hand, knows that the insured has paid to have financial protection available when he or she requires it. There is no good guy / bad guy mentality. There is just the necessity to understand the requirements of the policyholder in time of need and to resolve those needs as expeditiously as possible.

The lesson here is that strategy must precede values. There must be a conscious choice of strategy, and then there can be a discussion of the values and behavior required to support the strategy.

Let's take another example where setting values before understanding and choosing strategy would have been a mistake.

This time, consider the development of a strategic plan for a highly successful, family owned packaging company. The worst thing the owner could have done would have been to set values for the enterprise as the first step in the process. Instead, the owner undertook a study of the hows, why, and rationale of current strategy.

The findings were quite striking.

The business had two sides. One team focused on "dirty work," producing huge sheets of heavy-duty, waxed paper that was to be used for wrapping large new machines for shipping domestically and abroad. The other team did "clean work," producing paper for the food industry.

These two teams had to share the plant floor and, at times, the same packaging production equipment.

Think about the conflicting values in the two teams as they generated their respective product lines.

The heavy machinery folks worked with large sheets of industrial paper. They did not worry about perfect sheets. They covered the sheets in wax. This was the value-added step that made their product attractive to their heavy equipment clients.

Meanwhile, the other team worried about hygiene and perfection. The products they produced were for use in packaging and serving food. One of the teams and its line had to go. The conflict in values was apparent both on the shop floor and in management meetings.

Once the owner chose which line to keep, then the owner was able to sit down and articulate the values that had made that line of business such a success.

Alpha Strategy Informing Values

Another way to look at the flaws in the way we identify values today is to map them to The Alpha Strategies.

If we take the typical values we see hanging on the reception area wall or the splash page of most organizations, what we see are values associated with the organization management strategy.

Think of the typical list of values. It usually includes statements on honesty, being a team player, respect, the need for interpersonal skills, a commitment to service excellence, the need to be cost conscious, a bias toward continuous improvement, and a community focus.

We think all these values can be mapped to the organization management strategy. They do not map easily to any of the other strategies.

Figure 27 Mapping Typical Value Statements to Alphas

THE ALPHA STRATEGIES	CONTENT	VALUE AS EXPECTATION
BUSINESS DEFINITION	FOCUS ON BUSINESS POSITIONING IN THE EXTERNAL ENVIRONMENT	APPLICABILITY?
RISK	FOCUS ON THE UNACCEPTABLE	APPLICABILITY?
GROWTH	FOCUS ON SIZE	APPLICABILITY?
FINANCIAL MANAGEMENT	FOCUS ON SOURCING, ALLOCATION AND MANAGEMENT OF CAPITAL	APPLICABILITY?
R+D / TECHNOLOGY	FOCUS ON CREATION AND/OR USE OF INTELLECTUAL CAPITAL	APPLICABILITY?
ORGANIZATION MANAGEMENT	FOCUS ON SOURCING, ALLOCATION AND MANAGEMENT OF HUMAN RESOURCES	HONESTY; TEAM PLAYER; RESPECT; INTERPERSONAL SKILLS; SERVICE EXCELLENCE; COST CONSCIOUS; CONTINUOUS IMPROVEMENT; COMMUNITY FOCUS
MARKETING	FOCUS ON SOURCING AND CAPTURING CUSTOMERS / CLIENTS	APPLICABILITY?
SERVICE DELIVERY / PRODUCTION / MANUFACTURING	FOCUS ON FULFILLING MARKETING PROMISE	APPLICABILITY?

The fact that statements of values commonly used in most organizations are focused entirely on organization management reinforces our belief that there is still a lot of work to be done on articulating values to support the implementation of the remaining seven strategies.

And even the values commonly articulated for organization management strategy sound so empty and unhelpful. It is because, for the most part, these values are stating the obvious. Why would anyone want to work at an organization where there was no honesty or integrity? Or respect for fellow employees? Or team work and basic civil behavior? The typical values do little more than identify the minimum behavior expectations to be met by prospective employees seeking to work at an organization.

Let's look at some great organizations that have clearly used a deep understanding of their alpha strategy to articulate their values.

We'll start with IBM since the list of its values, as stated on its website, is breathtakingly short: dedication to every client's success; innovation that matters, for the company and the world; and trust and personal responsibility in all relationships.

First, and most obvious: these three values are not enough by themselves to guide implementation of strategy. Former CEO Sam Palmisano said as much on the IBM website in 2003 when announcing these three values. IBM, he observed, would bring these values to life in its policies, practices, and daily operations.

Can you imagine how many policies, procedures, and rules there are at IBM? This is a company of 427,000 folks all over the world. When an IBM consultant makes a simple sales call, he or she has received training not only on how to sell, but also on the relevant policies and procedures within the sales process so that he or she will perform the sales call in the manner IBM expects.

This is a company with one hundred years of history. I can remember hearing that the uniform at IBM used to be a dark suit: usually blue, with a white shirt, and sombre tie. Shoes were to be black Oxfords with laces and four eyelets, not three. You can feel the values at that time coming alive in just the uniform that IBMers wore to work. Apparently, the purpose was to look like the management at IBM's big customers. This was the uniform of the IBM manager. The belief was that if you looked serious, the customer will take you seriously.

To see if the alpha drives articulation of values at IBM today, let's look at the firm's alpha. We have made the case that we think the alpha is business definition, the strategy of ongoing market positioning. It is the strategy that answers Drucker's question, "What is our business?"

We can paraphrase the IBM business definition strategy this way: an ongoing focus on high value, high growth segments of information technology.

We believe that this is the strategy that CEO Palmisano keeps referring to as transformational. IBM seems to be continually morphing, just like the popular pop singer Madonna, to stay relevant and thriving. IBM does this by always stretching into the emerging attractive segments of IT and exiting businesses that are becoming low value and commoditized.

This is the "morphing strategy" that we think Lou Gerstner put in place when he took over a troubled IBM in 1992 and shifted it away from a manufacturing alpha. He started a change in culture that took more than ten years to complete.

By 2003, the company wanted to articulate its core values. Maybe this was because Mr. Palmisano had recently taken over as CEO and wanted a way to put his mark on the company. For whatever reason, the company undertook an online, virtual process that solicited input on the values that were contributing the most to IBM's success. Three values were identified.

The first IBM value speaks to understanding each client's needs thoroughly. This is something that opens a window onto the client organization's world and reveals where the customer is heading and how it is changing. Arguably, this value could speak to either business definition or marketing, except we believe it informs decision making on the next shift in business definition.

The second value speaks more clearly to business definition by addressing the need for "innovation" or change. For IBM, it is change that matters, and by measuring it against change important to the world, it shows it to be very big change indeed.

Finally, there is the third value, trust and personal responsibility. Again, this seems to flow from the alpha of business definition because it is the individual employee's responsibility to embrace and adapt to change. This is the value that keeps folks going when they don't always understand the change that is occurring but do accept that it is their personal responsibility to adapt to the change.

What I like about the IBM values story is that you can see that the change in strategy that Lou Gerstner launched in 1993 has given rise to the three values—*not the other way around.*

It was more than ten years until employees could articulate a new set of values. These are not the values employees aspire to. These are the values currently in place. The values that come out of an organization's alpha strategy should ideally be so recognizable, so palpable, that potential new employees take them in and know instantly whether they want to join the organization or run, not walk, away from it.

Let's look, for example, at the values of Lands' End, the venerable catalog and now online retailer. As a retailer, it has marketing as its alpha strategy.

Founder Gary Comer summed up its marketing strategy this way: "Our basic premise for winning customers is little different today than when we started. Sell only things we believe in, ship every order the day it arrives, and unconditionally guarantee everything. That was, and still is, the platform."

Alpha strategy at Lands' End is marketing, while an influencer is service delivery. Because of this clear understanding of alpha strategy, the company has been able to articulate its "values and practices," the basic premise of which is that what is good for the customer is good for Lands' End.

This is easy to say but hard to implement. Hard, that is, unless everyone in the firm believes in the values and practices them.

CHAPTER 8
ALPHA IMPACT

Four Essays on Current Popular Beliefs in Strategy

The impact The Alpha Strategies has on current notions of strategy is significant. We are going to argue that the approach proves the old saw, "Strategy before structure" is correct. It is nonsense to think that people come first and then we design strategy to suit the people we have.

We are going to argue that there is always a strategic plan in every organization. This is because the eight strategy framework is inherent in every organization that is up and running. Whether those strategies have been documented or not, we argue that they are nevertheless in existence.

We are going to argue that process (a synonym for strategy in our opinion) plays a far greater role than metrics. This is not to say that metrics don't play an important role. It is just that we are not comfortable that the right things are being measured. We know that numbers do not tell the whole story. Process and the hows and why of strategy implementation is what demands our focus.

Finally, we are going to argue that decision-making on strategy needs to be based on facts and the proper analysis of facts. There is no place for intuition in strategy. Intuition is just a fancy way to say "I don't know what I am looking at, but it feels familiar." Better to say the latter than the former and, in particular, to be saying the "I don't know" part. Otherwise, you, as a decision maker, run the risk of being delusional; meaning making a decision *when you don't know that you don't know* what you are supposed to do.

Strategy Comes First, Please. Then People.

There is a popular misconception that all that is needed to pull together a strategic plan is to get the "right" people working on it.

While we can understand why putting the "best and the brightest" on the task might seem like common sense, we want to explore this myth further because it reveals a complete lack of understanding of how strategy first comes into being and how expectations drive all subsequent strategy planning.

To understand how The Alpha Strategies first come into being, we have to look at an organization that is just being founded.

We are going to use the urban legend about the founding of Apple to construct a story to describe our notion on how each of The Alpha Strategies comes into being and the role Steve Jobs and Steve Wozniak, the founders of Apple, had in strategy creation.

For those of you who don't know the story, it goes something like the following.

Steven Jobs and Steven Wozniak (and a third person whose name, like that of the fifth Beatle, has disappeared over time) get together and decide to set up Apple in 1976.

Breathing life into Apple started with the people. In effect, organization management was the first strategy of the eight to be set. The strategy was that all the tasks in the new organization would be divided up among the two Steves and the third co-founder.

Next was agreement on a marketing strategy. This was easy for Jobs and Wozniak because they had already decided that Apple was going to market personal computer kits to individuals who wanted to have a personal computer in their homes.

Unfortunately, none of the young entrepreneurs had any money or a place to build their revolutionary product. They decided to approach Jobs' father for a loan and the use of the family garage.

In other words, the financial management strategy was to borrow from Mr. Jobs Sr. Remember, this was all happening shortly after Ken Olson, president and founder of Digital Equipment Corporation (DEC), had famously declared: "There is no reason anyone would want a computer in their home." Having no doubt heard of Ken Olson's dismissal of the demand for personal computers, Steve's father probably wanted to hear his son explain how this new venture, called Apple, would be positioned in the computer industry before making a final decision on the loan and the use of the family garage.

In other words, the dad wanted the Steves to describe their business definition strategy.

The young Steves no doubt impressed Mr. Jobs Sr. with their detailed opinion of the total absence of competitors in their chosen business segment and the wide-open market for personal computers with its potential for spectacular growth. The dad was clearly sold on the idea because he lent them money and let them use the garage.

Next, the young men set the production strategy, which was to build their dream machine, the Apple personal computer, one computer kit at a time.

However, they quickly realized they could not produce product quickly enough to meet the demand. In effect, the young entrepreneurs were having their first experience with the risk strategy and the need to focus on threats and opportunities their company's strategies faced. The risk they identified was that using a custom shop approach was inappropriate when demand for the product required a high-volume production strategy.

They turned to the seventh strategy to be set, the technology strategy, to manage the risk. They moved production from the garage into a proper manufacturing setting complete with the technology of assembly lines, conveyors, and the associated usual practices to enable volume production.

The rest of the Apple story becomes a history of incredible global success. Apple changed the way we use personal computing in our lives. Apple took off. The growth strategy, being internal growth, was a happy consequence of the success of Jobs and Wozniak had in selling Apple personal computers.

As for "Which comes first? People or Strategy?", I would suggest that, having decided on the basic strategies they were going to pursue, the two Steves then went looking for the right people to implement those strategies. So, with the exception of setting the initial strategies for an organization, people come second.

We can see from the Apple story that the Steves, being the owners and founders of the company, were the key to setting strategy initially. After that, the requirements of their chosen strategies become paramount in choosing the right people to implement them. The relevant issue becomes "How do we know what skills and experience we need in order to ensure successful implementation?" The answer to this question can only come from setting the strategy first.

There is yet another fallacy in the notion that people come first in setting strategy. It is the idea that managers are free to develop whatever strategy they want. That is the inference we take from the advice to put "the best and brightest" in a room and they will develop acceptable strategy. In reality, all strategy implementation planning is done by reference first to expectations and constraints imposed on the planning team by the strategy they are expected to implement.

Rarely do these expectations include the freedom to "just blue sky it." Anyone who has worked has experienced these constraints. The fact the constraints exist at all is further evidence that strategy has come first and that the folks responsible for implementing it must acknowledge that strategy.

The initial setting of strategy also includes choosing the alpha or lead strategy and positioning of the influencers and enablers. This choice is typically only made by the founders of the company. We believe that the choice of alpha strategy for an organization represents a major point of differentiation between for-profit organizations, on the one hand, and not-for-profits and the public sector, on the other.

In the private sector, we think the choice of alpha typically reflects the personality and choice of the founder. With Apple, it is possible to see how the marketing genius of Steve Jobs resulted in marketing becoming the alpha at Apple. With Intel, makers of computer chips, we think the choice of the alpha of R&D / technology reflects the research genius of its founders, Gordon Moore, Robert Noyce, and Andrew Grove. Isadore Sharp founded the Four Seasons hotel chain on a vision of extraordinary service, which we think made the alpha, service delivery.

In the not-for-profit and public sector, alpha strategy typically flows from a political process. A need is identified through that political process and an organization is created to address that need. Alpha strategy is set on a basis consistent with that need. A service delivery mandate demands a service delivery alpha. A regulatory mandate demands a risk alpha.

A leader should then be chosen to head the organization because of his or her perceived skills and track record in managing the chosen alpha strategy.

Every Organization has a Strategic Plan

The second issue The Alpha Strategies model dismisses very quickly is any notion that "We don't have a strategic plan." There is always a strategic plan in every organization. It just may not be in writing.

Almost every book and article on strategy planning, by far the majority of folks who attend my courses, and almost everyone I meet to talk to about planning seems to believe that an organization that has no strategic plan document has no strategies and no plan.

The reality is that every organization that is up and running is implementing its unique set of The Alpha Strategies. If employees and managers are showing up for work, services being delivered, and so on; then the Alpha Strategies are present and being implemented.

This is certainly the common understanding among competitive intelligence researchers. We don't stop our research on a target organization simply because we cannot find any evidence of a written strategic plan. We research the strategies being implemented and build what we assume is the strategic plan based on our findings on those strategies. The fact that a written strategic plan doesn't exist doesn't mean there isn't a plan or strategies.

Very few cities had a written strategic plan before the practice became popular or it became mandatory to produce one beginning around the 1990s. I sure can identify dozens of major cities that were in business long before the 1990s and managed to deliver services without that plan. I am hard-pressed to identify an entrepreneur who puts his or her strategy to paper until it becomes a requirement of a lender or some other third party. I certainly know lots of entrepreneurs running sizeable businesses who have never developed a strategic plan. All this tells me is that they haven't bothered to put their strategies to paper.

And, quite frankly, when I look at what we are told is the "right" way to develop a strategic plan I can understand why so many folks running their own businesses can't be bothered to do it.

The average person's impression of the preparation of a strategic plan is something that takes months and months to develop and starts with mystical processes such as divining "core values and principles" and "mission statements" and "visioning". And everyone has their own opinion of what constitutes a strategy or an objective or a mission statement.

The reality is that strategic planning should begin with capturing a description of each of the eight strategies of The Alpha Strategies presently being implemented. This is something that can be done in less than one hour by an entrepreneur or indeed, most executive management.

Getting agreement on those descriptions from the rest of the management team might be a whole other matter. Getting into detailed descriptions of the way those strategy descriptions are actually being implemented might take even more time. But getting started with agreement on what the summary description is for each of The Alpha Strategies has to be the starting point. It is the only way I know to conduct a reality check on the assumption that everybody understands what those strategies are.

I think all boards should have a recurring agenda item to discuss one of each of The Alpha Strategies at each board meeting. That way, board members could develop a deep understanding of current strategy, the risks it faces, and the values and expectations driving strategy implementation. Why ever do we have this practice of talking about strategy once a year at a board retreat? Who can assimilate all that information in one session?

I would like to think what is really meant by the folks who say "We don't have a strategic plan" is either "We don't have a written strategic plan document" or "I don't agree with the strategies we are pursuing."

That is a completely different matter because it suggests a starting point for discussing and reaching consensus on strategy.

I can remember a young fellow who came up to me during one of my courses. He said to me "Alan, I am going to tell my CEO that we need a strategic plan! I have been working for him as his assistant for over a year now and I have never seen it."

I said to him "Slow down. What makes you think he doesn't have one?"

The young fellow replied "Well, if he does, he's never shared it with anyone. And I just don't think he has one."

To this, I asked "How long has your company been in business?"

He said "Seventy-five years. We have offices in three countries and send our product all over the world."

"And you really think all of that is happening with no plan in place?" I asked.

"Well" he said. "What do you think I should do?"

To which I told him "You should sit down and write out your best understanding of each of the eight alpha strategies being implemented, including how they are configured into the alpha, influencers, and enablers. Talk to others in the company. When you are satisfied with what you have, you should sit down with the CEO and ask him if he would review your descriptions because you want to know if they are reasonably correct. If he asks why you are doing this, you can say that you want to develop a better understanding of the company's strategies and the way it does business because it will help you do your job better."

I told him that, in my experience, the CEO would either give him a copy of the strategic plan or, if one truly didn't exist, the CEO would very likely become interested in the draft strategy descriptions. If there is one subject that holds the CEO's attention, it is talking about the strategies of the organization. Finally, I told him that the worst that could happen was that the draft descriptions eventually became the organization's first strategic plan. Not a bad ending at all, considering where the discussion started.

There are two points being made here. The first point is that if an organization is up and running, the Alpha Strategies are being implemented and can be described. The trick is to capture descriptions of those strategies and to document how the strategies are configured into the alpha, influencers, and enablers. The second point is that capturing descriptions of existing strategy is the starting point for all strategy planning. It is problematic to propose changes to strategy without knowing what the present strategy is.

I always start my three day strategy course by pointing out that there is invariably someone attending the course that is under a lot of pressure to deliver a strategic plan, usually the day after the course! I assure that person, whoever she or he might be, that in twenty-five years of preparing strategic plans, I could categorically say that unless she knew already what changes in strategy were being contemplated, her presentation should be one of the existing strategy and, maybe, if there was time, an identification of the external factors impacting the performance of those strategies.

Unfortunately, this is not what we are told by most of the "planning experts". They would have us believe that planning is a problem to be solved. As a result, a lot of planning starts with identifying a problem and then proposing solutions. This approach is flawed for many reasons. First, strategy is not a problem to be solved. Strategy is a choice of action based on an understanding of factors outside of the control of the strategy planner.

Second, the focus on a problem quickly becomes a focus on a specific strategy when it is all eight that should be the subject of the review.

Third, without consensus on the description of present strategy, including the configuration of strategy into alpha, influencers, and enablers, providing the rationale for change of strategy becomes problematic because there is no context for the change.

The Alpha Strategies provides the framework to capture descriptions of present strategy. The Alpha Strategies is the starting place for strategic planning. Hopefully, use of The Alpha Strategies approach will forever end the thinking that "We don't have a plan" and put the focus on reviewing the appropriateness of current strategy against factors in the external environment.

Process is Everything

We have no particular interest in metrics or strategy performance measures. It seems to us that most organizations spend more time on measuring things than trying to understand what its people are actually doing.

I am not comfortable that most organizations measure the right things. In most organizations, measuring means managing the results. What we should be doing is managing the process, not the results.

The only way we believe it is possible to understand what should be measured is to understand strategy and underlying activities better. The future of strategy lies in more and more focus on the hows and whys of strategy; not on results. There is still far too much playing with the numbers and not enough understanding of what is actually happening, such as the trade-offs and consequences of choosing metrics.

The future of strategy will, in our opinion, involve a return to the principles of Peter Drucker and Stephen Covey and other business thinkers, who long ago debunked the popular management notion, "What gets measured gets done."

If Drucker had believed that, he would have called his book *The Results of Management* rather than *The Practice of Management*.

If Covey had believed it, he would have titled his book, *The Seven Results of Highly Effective People* instead of calling it, *The Seven Habits of Highly Effective People*. None of Covey's seven habits speaks to measuring anything.

Dov Seidman's 2007 bestseller *How We Do Anything Means Everything* explained the fallacy about focusing on measurements. For Seidman, what we are measuring may occasionally be useful. But the how we are doing things is much more important to understand.

Consider this story. Politicians in Canada worry about "wait" times for hip surgery. They agree that waiting times must become shorter. Guess what? Waiting times decline drastically. How did that happen? It happened at the expense of a whole bunch of other operations and procedures, for which people now wait longer. In other words, the results are not telling the whole story. How many similar stories can you think of?

Sports teams don't win games by determining the number of goals or touchdowns or baskets they are going to score in the next game and then setting that as their objective. They win because they *practice*! On game day, it takes players only a second to look at the scoreboard to confirm whether they are winning or losing.

To demonstrate the increasingly fallacious fixation on measuring results, I developed an exercise, called Process versus Results, for my executive education courses.

The ostensible purpose of the exercise is to demonstrate the three steps in developing strategy. The first step is gathering facts. The second is analyzing them. The third is choosing strategy. Actually, the objective of the exercise is to demonstrate that it is more important to understand the hows and why of strategy than to measure strategy. I point this out at the end of the exercise, once the participants understand the implications in choosing between strategy and results.

I give the class my definition of process and results. Process is synonymous with strategy while results are the same as metrics.

Step 1: Gathering the Facts

The question I ask each student is "In your opinion, what is the importance of a focus on results and a focus on process in your organization, scored on the basis of one to seven?"

I assign a score of from one to seven to each of process and results. A score of one means little or no focus on process or results. Four means no opinion on the subject either way. Seven means a very high focus is important.

Needless to say, this portion of the exercise takes the longest because gathering the facts is time-consuming. It is always the longest portion of a strategy planning exercise. I ask each person for an answer and a brief explanation.

Once they have all had a chance to speak and to give me their scores, I point out that fact gathering has taken three times as long as I had told them the whole exercise would take. I explain that the lesson to learn from the first step is that gathering the facts takes the most time in any effort to develop strategy.

In other words, it takes time to acquire the facts. I then ask the group, "Do you think we are allowing folks enough time, through training and otherwise, to become informed on the strategy they are to manage and to understand what they are expected to do in their jobs?"

The usual consensus answer is no.

When the results are all in, which I have captured on page after page of flip chart paper taped to the wall, I point out that, for a researcher, this is when the panic truly settles in. This is because the results of the survey look alarmingly meaningless.

"What does all this data mean?" is a feeling common to all researchers.

Step 2: Analyzing the Data

And so begins the second step in strategy development, analyzing the data to identify patterns and possible insights. Typically, what researchers do next is to return to the original premise of the study. In our case, the premise is a relationship between process and results.

We can use that premise to plot the results and become a starting point for analysis. The most popular visual in business today for mapping data has to be the Cartesian plane—that infamous 2x2 matrix that is so powerful for organizing information.

From a researcher's perspective, it is not clear at this point whether any useful insights will emerge from the findings. But at least the client will receive an impressive looking graphic displaying those results.

I then create a 2x2, as shown in the figure below, to map the findings, using the research issues of process and results to become the ends of the axes.

Figure 28 Process versus Results Map

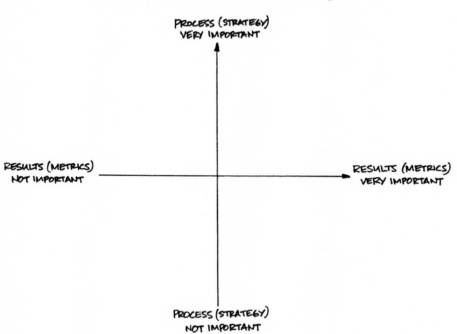

The horizontal axis is Results, with scores starting at 1 on the left hand starting point, "Focus on Results Not Very Important," through 4, where the axis crosses the vertical plane, to 7 at the right end of the axis, ". . . Very Important."

The vertical axis is Process. At the bottom of the axis, "Focus on Process Not Very Important" scores 1. There is a score of 7 at the top of the axis ". . . Very Important."

The end result is a Cartesian plane with four quadrants.

We then load the scores obtained from each of the participants into the appropriate quadrants. Most of the scores fit into the upper right quadrant, with both results and process "Very Important." Usually quite a few scores appear in the lower right quadrant, ". . . Results Very Important" and ". . . Process Not Very Important."

There are typically very few scores in either of the left quadrants. The results look as follows:

Figure 29 Loading in the Survey Responses

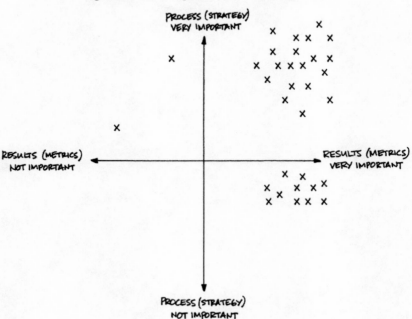

Just looking at the 2x2 with the scores loaded into it makes one wonder: what does it mean to be in the upper left quadrant or the lower right or, for that matter, any of the quadrants?

Now we are into the heart of the analysis. The scores aren't as important as understanding what it means to be in each quadrant.

I ask my students to work in groups to label each quadrant. When they are ready, we begin the discussion on what it means to be in each quadrant.

The Lower Left Quadrant: Red Ink

We start with the lower-left quadrant. The labels quickly identify the quadrant as a sinkhole for money and a recipe for bankruptcy because it devalues process and results. The best label I have heard: "red ink," i.e., bankruptcy.

The funniest comment: one participant felt his son's first year at university to qualify very much as a red-ink experience, what with the dad paying for everything and the son producing little more than expenses and failing grades.

Figure 30 The Red Ink Quadrant

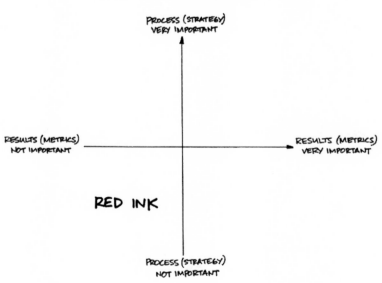

After all the laughing dies down, someone invariably asks, "Isn't it possible for a start-up to be in this quadrant?" I reply, "Absolutely!"

Already the class is seeing the beginnings of an organization's life cycle. I point out that the bottom right and upper right quadrants will flesh out that evolution.

The Lower Right Quadrant: Black and Blue

Next, we move to the lower right quadrant. In this quadrant, focus on process is not important, and results are everything. The general consensus of my groups is that this is the quadrant that entrepreneurs and start-ups occupy. Entrepreneurs are notorious for having the reputation that they do not care how results are achieved. Every day is a mad dash to "get it done."

My favorite label for the quadrant is "Black and Blue" for the bruising that everyone in such an organization endures with every day bringing a new crisis.

Figure 31 The Black and Blue Quadrant

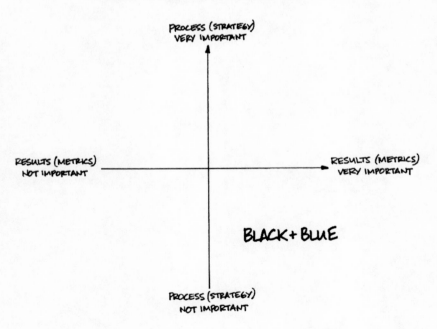

We can see how a start-up may struggle to find its legs in the bottom left quadrant and eventually find its way and build sufficient momentum to move into the bottom right.

The fancy consulting term "momentum" just means that start-up owners reach the stage where they no longer have to use their credit cards to meet payroll!

Their firm probably now has accounts receivable that secure an operating line [of credit?]. Maybe they have found an "angel" investor who has funded the start-up.

After time, the bottom right quadrant becomes unbearable.

It is such a waste of time and energy to manage recurring events as though they were unique and nonrecurring.

It is not productive to manage with such a short-term focus and mentality.

What usually happens is that the firm puts more and more process into place to increase productivity and encourage a longer term focus. As a result, over time the entrepreneurs finally break through into the upper right.

The Upper Right Hand Quadrant: Blue Sky

In the upper right hand quadrant, there is equal focus on process and on results.

This at first seems the perfect place to be. My groups often label the quadrant variously "Forbes 50" or "Blue Sky."

Figure 32 The Blue Sky Quadrant

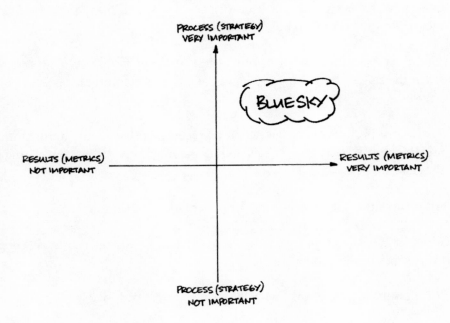

But I have a problem with the quadrant and its assumption that the perfect balance between strategy and metrics is the right way to manage an organization. This assumption defies everything I have ever seen. There is no such thing as a perfect balance. There is always only one priority and everything else is secondary. Either process or results must take precedence over the other. At best it is an uneasy truce, a détente, until a time comes to choose.

To test this premise, I ask my groups, "What happens when some event occurs that forces you out of the upper right quadrant?" I suggest examples, such as the bankruptcy of some major client or customer, a huge fraud by a rogue trader, the discovery of a defect that will force a major product recall, mad cow disease, or an oil rig explosion. These are all events that could threaten the firm's very survival.

There are now three choices. We can head back to black and blue, where no one cares how anyone does anything. The saying in that quadrant is "If there is a problem, just fix it. I don't care how you do it. Just do it."

This is a really scary place to be. "Just fix it" usually means at someone else's expense! The way to dispose of toxic chemicals is to dump them into an empty mine shaft on someone else's property during the dark of the night. This is a quadrant of questionable activities.

We think of Nick Leeson, the rogue trader in the Singapore office of Barings Bank, toiling away in this quadrant. No one in London head office seemed to want to know what he was doing to generate the profits he was producing, at least until the profits stopped and then turned to losses. This is the quadrant of WorldCom and Enron. Once folks found out *how* these guys were making money, there was an outcry.

The U.S. Congress then passed the Sarbanes-Oxley Act to force executives in public companies to certify quarterly, on pain of going to jail, that everything their company was doing was in compliance with all laws. I point out to my class the reality: "We cannot go back to black and blue unless we want to go to jail!"

Figure 33 The Choices of Action

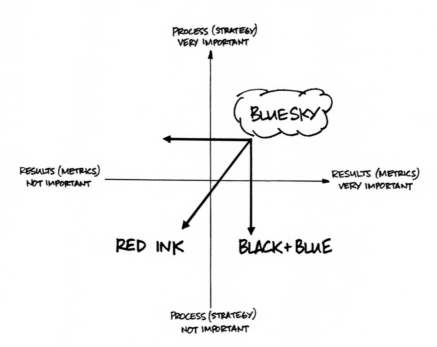

That leaves us with two choices. We could go to the bottom left quadrant, red ink. That would probably mean bankruptcy, never a happy choice. Or we could move into the upper left quadrant. If that is going to be a choice, then we had better understand what it means to be in that quadrant.

The Upper Left Hand Quadrant: Focus on Process

By process of elimination, the students generally choose the upper left. But many of them are uncomfortable because of the labels they have given the quadrant. This is the quadrant where results are not important and process is very important. The groups typically mention "analysis paralysis," "bureaucratic," "process improvement," and "red tape." I point out that process improvement seems different from the other characterizations.

That's when it becomes apparent that the quadrant divides into two segments. One involves bureaucracy and red tape, but the other smaller segment, which I call "true sustainability," scores perhaps 2 for focus on results and from more than 4 to 7 for focus on process.

Figure 34 Red Tape / True Sustainability Quadrant

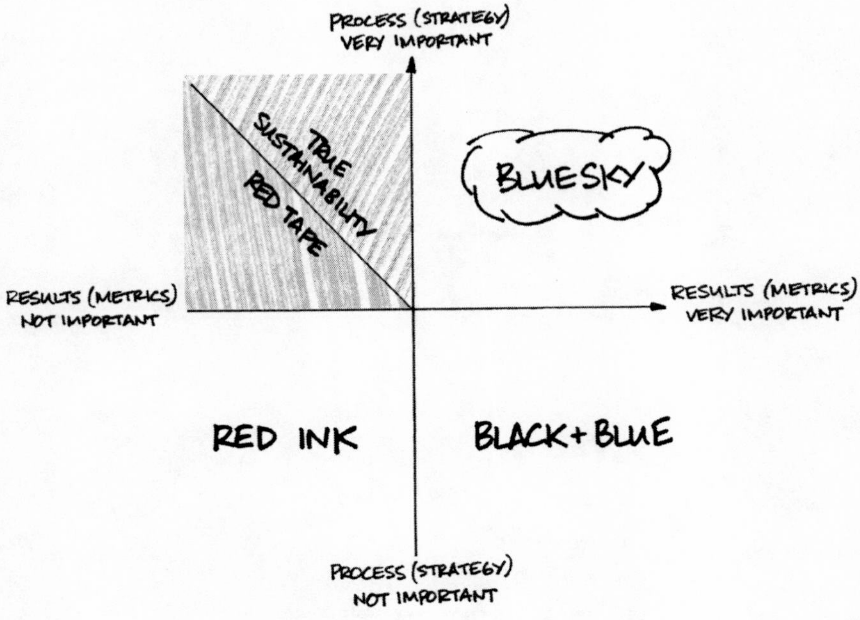

In the "True Sustainability" segment, there is much more focus on strategy and process than on results and metrics. There is no longer a balance between the two. This is because companies in this segment know that it is what they are doing that drives the results as opposed to what they measure. Therefore, they want to focus intensely on what they are doing.

If there is too much focus on process for its own sake, then process becomes the "red tape" and bureaucracy, which we want to avoid because it adds no value.

As an example, I tell the story that when Michael Dell retook the CEO's role at Dell Computers in 2007, it was because the company was struggling. His first e-mail to every employee was: "We have a new enemy. That enemy is bureaucracy. If we don't defeat it, we will lose the company."

Michael Dell understands that any organization, to be truly successful, must function in the upper segment of the upper left quadrant of true sustainability. This is because this is the only quadrant of sustainable change.

That's the secret to Dell's success; its ongoing focus on process, not on results. That's the power of lean manufacturing and the Toyota Way. When Toyota could not keep up its focus on process because it was growing too fast then the recalls and defects started.

The future of strategy lies in the true sustainability segment. Companies need to be constantly managing the hows and why of implementation.

Metrics can fool us into taking our eye off the hows and why of strategy if we don't constantly confirm our understanding as to how the metric emerged.

Step 3: Making Strategy Choices
We have now finished the analysis and can enter step 3. Step 3 is about making a decision on which of the strategy choices seems the most attractive to pursue. We review the choices, being red ink, black and blue, blue sky, and the upper left hand quadrant choices of red tape and true sustainability. These are the choices of action.

Figure 35 The Five Strategy Choices

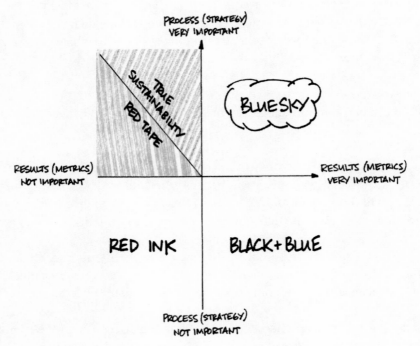

The exercise has shown us that the likely evolutionary path of a start-up as it grows into a successful organization will see it move from red ink, through the black and blue quadrant then on to blue sky to true sustainability. But as to making a decision, all the exercise has done is show us the choices and the importance of analyzing the facts in order to come to an informed decision.

From my perspective of using The Alpha Strategies as the framework to understand current strategy and the factors impacting strategy, I see far too many organizations sitting in the bottom right hand quadrant but patting themselves on the back because they think they are in the upper left.

I suggest that the truly high performing companies, such as IBM and Goldman Sachs, are well entrenched in the upper left hand quadrant of "true sustainability".

Are You Making Delusional Decisions?

While we are on the topic of decision making, let me confirm that there is a process for reaching a decision. Let's slow down the process and see how the elements of time, facts, and understanding relate to each other.

Please note that we are not actually going to make a decision. That would involve discussing decision heuristics, being all the influences on making a decision. We are just going to see how people should reach a position to make a decision, in my opinion.

In my executive education classes, I use an exercise called Facts versus Understanding to demonstrate what is at play in the process leading up to making a decision.

The two obvious elements are facts and understanding: facts, being our perception of the facts and what we think we need to know or think we know.

And then there is understanding, being the thinking that we understand those facts and are able to make an informed decision using that understanding.

I use another Cartesian plane to depict the relationship between these two factors.

The horizontal axis runs from "Think we do not have sufficient facts" to "Think we have sufficient facts."

The vertical goes from "Do not think we understand the facts" to "Think we understand the facts."

We will work our way through the quadrants counterclockwise from the bottom left, trying to label each one.

Figure 36 Facts versus Understanding Map

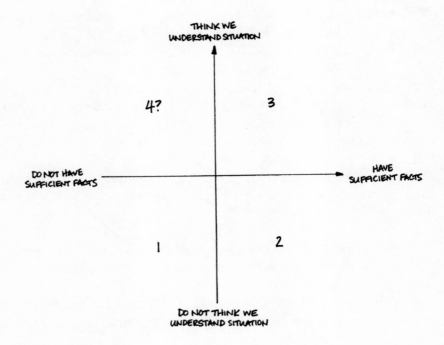

Starting in the bottom left, quadrant 1, we think we do not have the facts, and we think we do not understand the facts.

What label best describes this quadrant? At first, the conclusion might be that we have lost our way, that we are sinking, or that the situation is hopeless.

My students all admit to having some familiarity with these feelings, having experienced them at one point or another in their careers. In reality, this quadrant represents where we are in terms of our critical thinking on the first day of a new job!

That's why I think the best description of the quadrant is "Day 1."

Figure 37 Day One Quadrant

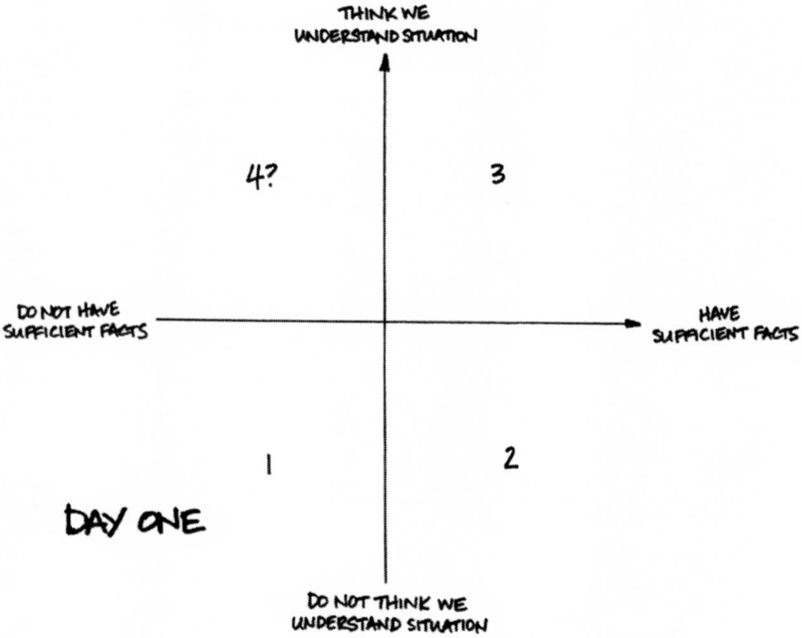

Do you remember your first job?

You probably spent the day in an anxious state. The major achievement of the day was finding the washrooms! You didn't know when or where to go for lunch or even how long to take. You did find the coffee machine. You weren't sure what time you should leave. As your career unfolded, you began to accept this quadrant and the sinking feelings that come with it, as a normal consequence of the arrival of each new assignment, promotion, transfer, and project you receive.

So much for explaining the facts and understanding aspects of the quadrant, let's look at the time element.

From a time perspective, quadrant 1 could be called the "honeymoon phase." The amount of time you get to linger there varies tremendously from organization to organization. But one thing is for sure: you can't stay there forever.

As you go about collecting information on your job, you are actually moving along the horizontal axis. With each additional piece of learning, you are also climbing up the vertical axis. At some point, you find your journey of learning has taken you into the bottom right into quadrant 2.

Figure 38 Moving to the Lower Right hand Quadrant

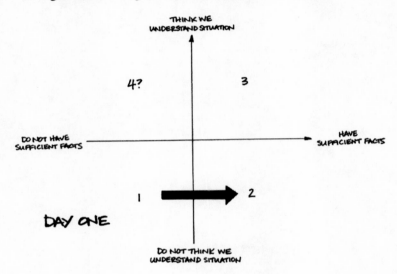

In quadrant 2, we think that we have enough facts, but we don't think that we understand them.

My students offer various labels to describe the quadrant, ranging from "analysis paralysis" to "hire a consultant" to "recheck the facts." All of these labels suggest the unease that comes from knowing you should be able to make a decision but can't quite bring yourself to do so. This makes you appreciate the bliss of ignorance you experienced in the bottom left quadrant. Why? Because now you *know* that you have the facts.

The pressure comes from *not knowing if you understand what the facts are and what your analysis of the facts should be telling you.* There is pressure on you because you, as a manager, know or at least live in fear that someone else, usually someone who wants your job or your next promotion or your best customer or client or, worse still, your boss, is going to understand the facts before you do. When that happens, the other person's usual reaction is "What do we need you for if we are figuring it out before you are?"

This is the quadrant of paranoia. It is also where most of us will spend the majority of our careers! So get used to it! This is life in the workplace. We are paid to think about what we should be doing. If we are managers, we are paid to inform ourselves and then to develop sound choices of action.

My best label for this quadrant is "your job."

I think quadrant 2 is the focus of Andy Grove's *Only the Paranoid Survive* (1999). Grove was cofounder of Intel and has written extensively on management and strategy. This book looks at how changing external factors force rethinking of strategy. From a time perspective, occupants of quadrant 2 already have all the relevant information and analysis they need to make decisions. The only time they need is more time to conduct further analysis and look at choices of action. This always takes far less time than learning all the facts.

Figure 39 "Your Job" Quadrant

And then there is the upper right quadrant 3, where we think we have sufficient facts and also think we understand them.

Figure 40 Moving to the Upper Right hand Quadrant

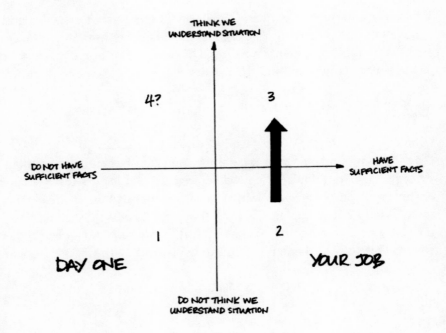

Sounds like bliss, doesn't it?

What usually happens is something like this. You have traveled from quadrant 2 to quadrant 3 to pitch your boss on an idea or recommendation. Even before you have finished, he or she is furiously working the keys on his or her BlackBerry and looks up and says, "Great idea. I'm launching it right now!"

And all you can think is that you want to run back to your laptop and recheck, for the fiftieth time, your assumptions and projections.

But it is too late, the boss has decided! This is the quadrant of "the executive decision."

Figure 41 The "Executive Decision" Quadrant

From a time perspective, a decision truly occurs in a heartbeat. That's why my favorite definition of an executive decision is "A decision made in a nanosecond after days or weeks or months of debate and agony."

We can now see that becoming knowledgeable, moving from the bottom left quadrant to the bottom right, probably took the most time.

Moving from the bottom right to the top right doesn't take nearly as long because being in the bottom right means always being ready to make a decision. It's just that sometimes we want to delay that with more due diligence or, sometimes, procrastination.

The consequence of a really great decision in the upper right quadrant is a promotion or a transfer or new accounts or a new project. In other words, more! This puts you right back into quadrant 1. That's right—back to no facts and no understanding!

The consequence of a more typical, business-as-usual decision is return to quadrant 2, your job.

Figure 42 Consequences of a Good Decision

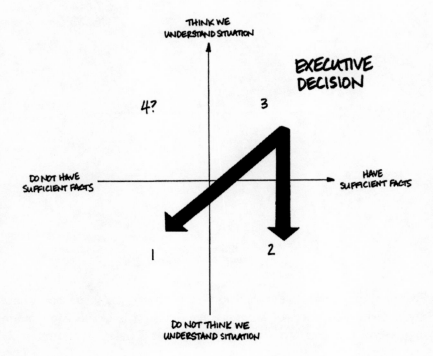

And that's life at work: a never-ending continuum of paranoia, successful decision making, learning, and every now and then, starting over in quadrant 1.

Now we need to turn our attention to quadrant 4. In this quadrant, we think we understand the situation but do not have sufficient facts. What is going on?

Figure 43 The Upper Left hand Quadrant

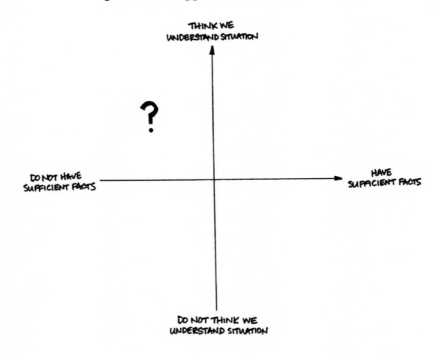

At first, not having the facts and thinking one understands the facts looks delusional. This is certainly what my students say when I ask them for a label for the quadrant. However, they struggle to reconcile that characterization with the admission that most of them have found themselves in quadrant 4 at one time or another.

Some of them point out that the facts are not always going to be available, yet that shouldn't stop decision making.

When man went to the moon, the fact that no one had ever done it before did not stop NASA. NASA knew all about space travel and had practiced landings in locations with terrains similar to that on the moon. The point is that everyone at NASA understood that no one had ever landed on the moon. Therefore, there was no exact understanding of exactly what landing on the moon might entail.

That is the difference between being delusional and being rational. You are delusional if you proceed as if you understand the facts and do not know that you do not have the facts. You are rational if you admit that you know you do not have the facts. This admission frees you and the team around you to look for substitutes that might serve as adequate facts. These might come in the form of a like situation.

Perhaps the most memorable examples of delusional decision making I have ever seen were on the videos of pilots in a flight simulator trying to fly out of major accidents that had occurred at the airline.

It was 1980 and industry participants decided to study a number of catastrophic crashes suffered over recent years. Part of the study involved videotaping how the cockpit crew worked together in an emergency. The cause turned out to be the mentality of World War II veterans who, by the 1970s and 1980s, were senior enough to be piloting big jets.

Watching the flight simulator videos, the researchers found that the vets were unable or unlikely to be able to work as a team with the copilot and the navigator when trouble hit. Instead, they would seem to ignore the facts and advice and attempt to solve the problem themselves. In one particularly terrifying video clip, the copilot advises the pilot that there isn't sufficient fuel to make the maneuver the pilot is making. The pilot dismisses his colleague's concerns as nonsense. The plane then crashes before it reaches the runway, just as the copilot had predicted.

In another clip, involving loss of power to two engines shortly after takeoff, the captain, who is not a war veteran, asks his team for suggestions after nothing on the checklist of standard procedures works. It is the navigator who suggests using the onboard auxiliary power units (APUs).

A bit of back story is necessary. First, since the late 1980s, there have been no navigators on jets. And even at the time of this video, pilots and copilots tended to treat the navigator as part of the cabin crew, fit to fetch coffee, but not to comment on flight matters. Second, the APU provided onboard power to the aircraft on the ground and was not intended for use in the air.

Nevertheless, in the video the pilot listens to the advice and then asks the copilot if he agrees. The copilot replies that he can see no reason why the idea wouldn't work. The pilot asks, "So we all agree?" "Yes," the other two reply. "Then let's start the APU," orders the pilot. The APU kicks in, starting the first failed engine, which fires up successfully. And then the second engine starts up. Needless to say, the team is jubilant. And the crew flies out of a situation that could have killed everyone on board.

When making decisions in quadrant 4, the difference between being and not being delusional is recognizing explicitly when there are no facts. Substitutes for facts can come into play, such as experience from similar situations or from extrapolation or from experience.

According to urban legend, when Silicon Valley was focused on building the Internet in the 1980s, apparently a bestselling reference book in the valley was about the history of the construction of the American railroad.

I can only think that bright minds in the valley were reaching for anything that would give them a sense of what they were undertaking. They had no facts to support their decision making on what they were going to do. They had to reach for substitutes.

While no one had ever built the Internet before, there was a railroad in place. The analogies between the two are obvious. There are main tracks, towns and cities along the way, various types of railroad cars carrying various things, and so on. It was an excellent template, if not perfect, for imagining what the internet would eventually look like and how it would operate.

It is when the manager *does not know that he or she does not know* that he or she has no facts to support decision making that delusion sets in.

If he accepts that he does not have the facts, then he can proceed to take a calculated risk.

For that reason, I split the upper left quadrant into two segments. One is "a calculated risk," where people know they do not have the facts and know they are using some sort of substitute that makes the most sense. The other is "delusional," where people make decisions without knowing that they don't know the facts.

This is shown in the figure below.

Figure 44 Delusional / Calculated Risk Quadrant

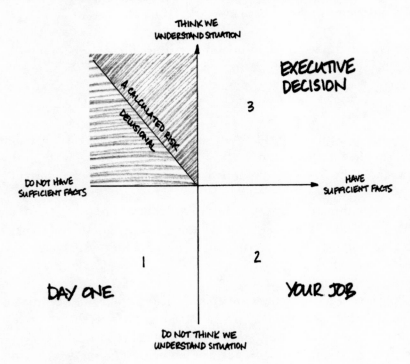

To recap, quadrant 1 is the start of knowledge in a new job or with a new file or account or project or promotion.

At some point comes entry to quadrant 2. The honeymoon is officially over, and the employee can make sense of the situation and help with decision making.

Quadrant 3 is about decision making. People stay there only briefly, because a decision takes but a moment.

Quadrant 4 involves the calculated risk and/or delusion.

I have used this exercise a lot in the classroom. Obviously, I apply it to make the point that gaining knowledge is the most time-consuming activity. This is the transition from quadrant 1 to quadrant 2.

I also emphasize that quadrant 2, being "Your Job", is not always a comfortable place to be. The pressure to act is constant in this quadrant.

Finally, the exercise is useful to demonstrate that making decisions without apparent facts will happen as a matter of course. The trick is to keep from being delusional by acting as though there *are* facts. There must be an explicit acknowledgment that there are no facts and that some reasonable substitute is taking their place.

I have also used the exercise as a one-on-one tool for counseling someone who is struggling with decision making.

The power of the tool is that it helps break down the existential human struggle with reaching the position to make a decision. The question becomes: which quadrant do you think you are in now, in your journey toward making a decision?

From The Alpha Strategies perspective, I think a whole lot of strategy planning and decisions are being made in the delusional segment of the upper left hand quadrant.

Folks are undertaking strategy planning with no understanding of the facts required, namely, the process, the facts on current strategy and its performance, stakeholder expectations, and the impact of external factors on strategy performance.

This to me is delusional because it results in strategy decisions not based on facts.

EPILOGUE

Takeaways for Our Readers

We wrote this book for a wide range of readers interested in strategy. Here is our take on what we are offering each group.

For directors of an organization, our model provides a means for a board to make better decisions when it undertakes its two fundamental responsibilities: the approval and then ongoing oversight of the organization's strategic plan.

The Alpha Strategies approach provides board members with the structure to understand the strategic plan and to assess the potential impact of any proposals to change it. The approach makes it possible for board members to understand better how a change in one strategy will impact the other strategies. Too often, strategy proposals to boards never provide this context.

For leaders of organizations of any size, from a sole proprietorship to a public company, from a department of government to a national not-for-profit, the model offers a powerful means for directing strategy and change. Understanding The Alpha Strategies enables leaders to identify the organization's culture and values. Understanding current strategy and its relationship to the culture of the organization is essential to successful implementation of strategy and management of change.

For employees, The Alpha Strategies model offers a powerful tool to make sense of their organization and to understand where they fit in the organization by identifying which of the eight strategies contains their functional role. My research on attendees of my courses reveals that more than half of managers and employees want better, clearer explanations of their organization's strategic plan. Unfortunately, they are tired of waiting for those explanations. The alpha model enables them to conduct their own analysis and reach their own conclusions. There is nothing that pleases me more than when someone in my courses comes up to me and says, "I think I have figured out our eight strategies and which one is the alpha. I am really looking forward to taking up this discussion with my boss."

For risk managers, the model offers a robust method for identifying and addressing risk. This is because identifying risk demands understanding which of the eight strategies is the lead or dominant strategy, the alpha, and how the remaining seven are organized behind that lead. The alpha model also recognizes risk as one of the eight strategies common to all organizations. Too many risk management practices are flawed because they treat risk as something not related to strategy and they do not recognize the role of dominant strategy in identifying and prioritizing risks.

For strategy communications professionals, the model presents a powerful means for communicating strategy choices and expectations for implementation. It breathes real life and meaning into often meaningless terms such as vision and mission statements by relating those terms to The Alpha Strategies.

For academics studying strategy, The Alpha Strategies model offers many intriguing new premises worthy of research. The following list represents a few of the possible projects.

- Should all financial services organizations have financial management as their alpha or dominant strategy?
- Should insurers and pension funds have risk as their alpha strategy?
- Is growth an appropriate alpha strategy for all enterprises or should it be limited to retailers selling to end users?
- Should growth ever be the dominant strategy of an organization?

- What is the implementation success rate for organizations that have tried to change their dominant strategy?
- What has been the success/failure rate for organizations that have chosen leaders who are a mismatch for the alpha strategy of the organization

For industry analysts and researchers on competitive intelligence, The Alpha Strategies approach provides a powerful framework for research. Researchers can use it to collect data on competitors, customers, and other industry participants in order to construct a compelling picture of strategy practices that will help them to understand better the organization that they have chosen to study.

We wish you all the best with your strategy planning and communication efforts.

GLOSSARY

Strategy
Strategy is a chosen course of action.

For all managers, the choices of action are influenced by the expectations imposed on them and by the realities of the external environment. This definition renders the entire present day lexicon for strategy to being nothing more than synonyms for strategy.

The vocabulary of strategy has become an intimidating collection of synonyms that add no value to strategy communication and, in fact, make strategy inaccessible and incomprehensible. Some of our favorite synonyms are listed below.

Standard Single-Word Synonyms for Strategy
Vision, mission, values, principles, purpose, goals, objectives, initiatives, programs, projects, tactics, plan, task, action, policy, procedure, system, process, mandate, priorities

More Imaginative Synonyms for Strategy
Thread, pathway, direction, action, approach, design, maneuver, method, proposition, scenario, scheme, course, pathway, road, direction, expectations, targets

Double-Barreled Synonyms for Strategy

Corporate objectives, business objectives, strategic objectives, grand strategy, game plan, overarching principles, grand design, strategic themes, strategic intent, guiding principles, strategic imperatives, strategic initiatives, strategic priorities, strategic goals, strategic purpose, strategic leadership, achievable vision, priority actions, action sequences

Triple-Barreled Synonyms for Strategy

Long term goals, results oriented objectives, pillars of prosperity, strategic building blocks, balanced scorecard objectives, results-centric leadership, codes of behavior, overarching master plan

Strategic Thinking

Strategic thinking is thinking about how to align factors outside the control of a manager with the responsibilities assigned to that manager.

For most of us, factors outside our control mean first, the expectations imposed on us by our boss; and second, the realities of our external environment. A manager's nightmare is that imposed expectations do not match the realities of the competitive environment.

Strategic thinking is comprised of two words. The first word, "strategic," is an adjective meaning "concerned with strategy." We have already defined strategy as being a label for the way managers choose to manage the activities assigned to them. The adjective, strategic, is being used to modify the second word, thinking. Thinking can be defined as the mental processing of information. Putting the two words together leads to the common sense conclusion that strategic thinking must be thinking about strategy.

This leads to the question, "What do managers think about when thinking about strategy?" Ask any manager this question and the off-the-cuff answer will be something like "Whatever I have to do to keep my boss happy!" If that's what managers are thinking about when they think about strategy, then they are thinking about how to meet the expectations their boss has imposed on them.

The only tools a manager has to satisfy those imposed expectations are the activities assigned to him or her to manage. All of which leads to the conclusion that strategic thinking is making connections between assigned activities and performance expectations imposed on the manager. Hopefully, those expectations are consistent with the expectations of the strategic plan. It is expectations that keeps all strategy in the organization aligned with the strategic plan.

Strategic Management

Strategic management is leveraging the strategic thinking of individuals in the organization.

"Strategic" is an adjective, meaning "concerned with strategy." Strategy has already been defined as being a description of a chosen course of action. The second word, management, commonly means taking charge of an activity. The plain English result becomes "managing strategy."

The question then arises: "How does one manage strategy?"

Common sense would suggest that managing strategy means managing the individuals responsible for strategy implementation rather than managing a planning process. And when thought about further, the most critical activity to be managed is the strategic thinking of those individuals (i.e., the way they "think" about strategy) to ensure that expectations imposed on them actually do influence the way those individuals execute the activities assigned to them.

Strategic Issue

A strategic issue is a question of strategy.

The question is "Should we replace or improve current strategy?"

"Strategic" is an adjective, meaning "concerned with strategy." Strategy has already been defined as being a description of a chosen course of action. The second word, issue, is a synonym for question. The common sense definition would have a strategic issue be a question of strategy.

Then the question becomes "What questions are there about strategy?" The most basic question is "Should we improve the execution of existing strategy or should we replace existing strategy with a new strategy?"

Strategic Plan

The strategic plan sets direction and expectations for all subsequent strategy planning and implementation throughout the organization.

It accomplishes this by reviewing The Alpha Strategies for the organization as a whole, including their configuration, against changing external factors and stakeholder expectations to determine whether those strategies and their configuration are appropriate.

Business Plan

A business plan is an alignment of imposed expectations with assigned responsibilities.

The term, the business plan, is almost as unhelpful as the term, strategic plan in that, in plain English, it means a "plan of business."

For all strategy planning, other than the strategic plan, the factors outside the control of the planner are the expectations imposed on the planner by the strategic plan and the realities of the planner's competitive environment. The factors inside the control of the planner are the functional responsibilities assigned to the business unit, department, division, or project, or functional management team.

A business plan can be defined as a description of the way functional responsibilities will be managed to achieve the expectations and priorities of the strategic plan.

Expectations

Expectations describe in broad terms a hoped-for outcome.

Vision

Vision, in the context of The Alpha Strategies model, is a description of the hoped for outcome resulting from the long term pursuit (10-20 years) of the alpha or dominant strategy as influenced and guided by one or more of the influencers.

Mission

Mission, in the context of The Alpha Strategies model, is the business definition strategy; being the mandate strategy for not-for-profits and public sector organizations.

Risk

Risk is any occurrence of the unacceptable arising from factors that cannot be controlled.

Values

Values, within the context of strategic management, are expectations imposed on managers and employees by the strategic plan. These expectations are focused on describing the characteristics that individuals are expected to exhibit in their behaviors and decision making as they carry out their responsibilities with respect to strategy implementation.

Culture

Culture, within the context of strategic management, is a synonym for values.

DRAWING LIST

INDEX

W

Wal-Mart, 35, 107, 122, 127, 133
Welch, Jack (*Winning, 2005*), 96, 102
WorldCom, 159

Z

Zimmerman, John and Benjamin
    Tregoe, (*Top Management Strategy:
    What It Is and How to Make It
    Work, 1980*), 40-41